G000065532

Incongruent

Travel, Trauma, Transformation

Melanie Sue

INKED
ELEPHANT
PUBLISHING HOUSE

Inked Elephant Publishing House, LLC A Social Impact Publisher Inkedelephant.org

Library of Congress Cataloguing-In-Publication Data Names: Melanie Sue Hicks

Title: Incongruent: Travel, Trauma, Transformation / Melanie Sue; Foreword by Jennifer Pastiloff.

Description: Colorado Springs: Inked Elephant, 2023

Identifiers: ISBN 978-1-959694-02-1

Subjects: LCCN: 2022950067

BISAC: BIOGRAPHY & AUTOBIOGRAPHY/ Personal Memoir | SELF-HELP/ Motivational & Inspirational | TRAVEL/ Special Interest/ Adventure

Printed in the United States of America

[Handwritten inscription:]

Jody

Thanks for making Cannes so much better

top. Love & Admiration

Mel Lea

To anyone whose life did not turn out quite like they thought it would.

To everyone who learned to love it anyway.

Contents

Foreword

I own a URL. I own many but this particular one is my pride and joy because it's the motto I try, and often fail, to live by. This one is DontBeAnAsshole.net (.com was taken.) The thing is, and I know you know this, as much as we can try and not be an asshole (especially to ourselves), we often are. Let's not even begin to talk about how people can be that way towards us, as well; or at least we can perceive them to be. And let me not even touch upon how life itself can be an asshole in this foreword. Why not go there, you may be asking, if it's so common, this predilection towards assholiness? Because within the chapters of the book you hold in your hands, you'll be reminded that life can be a real dick and we do not need to beat a dead horse. The following pages will simultaneously remind you that despite the beating of dead horses, relationships beginning and ending and beginning again, medical scares, hard goodbyes and the messing up that turned out to not be messing up at all, we survive. And, if we wake up, as Melanie did and continues to do, we thrive.

Every single one of us has a box of stories we carry in our soul. I think we have eight hundred boxes. A million. These stories are ever shifting, too. This may sound strange, as if they are living things with heartbeats and such. They are. As we grow, we often look back on our stories and see them in new light and appreciation and wonder. Details can change; that's what happens with memory, isn't it? The gist of us, however, the gristle of who we are, remains.   What we have experienced, what we have seen, what we have faced: we have the power to tell our story as we alchemize it. This does not mean changing facts; although lord knows I have told the story of my father's death more times than can be counted and I also know the story is different now than it was when I was nine or seventeen. This is what memory does. It morphs. We have to be able to bend with it.

Consider how heartbreak can make you feel like you want to die and then one day you find yourself telling the story and that feeling is gone; you are simply saying then this happened and then that happened. The event still occurred but your pain has been transformed and turned into whatever you have turned it into. It's become part of you, somewhere. That is what our stories do. And they must be shared so thank the gods of airplane miles and travel magazines that Melanie shares hers with us. We get to feel less alone and if you don't feel alone at times, come over and have dinner with me. I mean that. We need each other. All our stories matter. Whether you have ever felt alone or not, whether you have kids or not, whether you have been divorced or found love, or not. Doesn't matter. And for the record, you will feel as if you have taken all the trips Melanie has taken even if you have never been on an airplane, so there's that. The power of stories never ceases to amaze me.

I often the tell a story (and yes, I am sure the details change slightly with each retelling of this story) of my time working at the Newsroom Cafe in Los Angeles. This fourteen-year chapter of my life often feels like a blur of life in survival mode when I try and recall it, a time when I thought of myself as a walking dead person. I'm a recovering-ish bag lady. Meaning that I tend to carry it all with me all the time and by all I mean: everything. As in: if I carry it all then nothing will ever stray or leave me. I do better these days, I think. At the restaurant my friends in the kitchen would play pranks on me by putting things in my backpack like a frying pan, a coffee mug, a melon, toilet paper, another melon and so on. The funny part (and by funny I mean sad sad sad part) was that I would trudge home and carry that dumb bag long before I noticed. (I remember being thrilled because I was out of toilet paper, but also awestruck at how oblivious I was.) Years later as I wrote my first book *On Being Human*, I called this story "Carry Only What You Need" and this is something I aim to do daily. We just carry so much, don't we? All the things we think we need that we don't. All the beliefs and opinions and shoulds, both from others and our own selves. All I could think as I read this book was thank heavens I was not hiking through Nepal with that ridiculous backpack.

Over the last thirteen years, in my workshops, I have had the privilege of hearing the stories of thousands of survivor/thrivers. The thriver part was always there it was just overshadowed by the bully of fear and surviving. Together we asked fear to take a hike, at least for a few hours at a time. Together we put down the backpacks full of rocks, otherwise known as shame.

For every story of victory, I have witnessed a woman locked in her own cage. Cages of fear, insecurity, shame, not-enoughness, pain. Those so focused on the past or the future that they miss the present (raises hand as I did that for years and sometimes still do), so I will be damned if this book is not right on time, Melanie Sue.

In my own life, I pride myself on showing what real motherfucking life looks like in hopes others will feel safe to do the same. Yes, I made a hashtag of it (#realmotherfuckinglife) because I am that dorky. Pride myself on that too, thank you very much. We live in a world of carefully crafted social media and image control at all costs, and I decided on a hard no to remain living in that land. It was a non-negotiable. This inconsistency between how we often try to appear versus who we really are can be the kindling that ignites our feelings of unworthiness hidden just under the surface and sometimes not hidden at all. In my wacky workshops (another thing I pride myself on is my freedom to be wacky and weird), I make space for people to find insights on their version of real life. Whatever it means to them. Whatever it means to you. We get to say, just like Mel does here in this book.

In January of 2016, Melanie walked into my workshop in Tampa, Florida. She was quiet but present. She stayed engaged throughout, seemingly deep in her own reflections and like many that are drawn to my WW Workshops (WW = Wacky Weird), she seemed to also be in search of an intentional space to find, or reclaim, her sense of self. Years later as I got to know her, I learned some of the details of her life and of her trauma and subsequent childlessness that she was coming to terms with that day she walked into my orbit in Tampa. We would cross paths periodically and I watched and clapped and cheered from afar as she let her own voice out of its cage. The roar that her voice turned out to be is culminated in this body of work.

Incongruent is more than just a travel book or just a book about trauma. There is no just about any of this. This is a story so many of us share and it is written for those who had ideas about the path their lives would take (isn't that all of us?) and then one day, we look around and realize we aren't even close to living the life we thought we would or were told we should.

Incongruent is a book of life lessons wrapped in a cloak of adventure and who doesn't need some damn adventure? I mean like The Choose Your Own Adventure kind, which is this book. Like Melanie, I have often used the quiet time of a long plane ride to get lost in the clouds out the airplane window and reflect. Melanie uses her travel experiences to dive into her own vulnerability which allows us to dive into ours if we choose that particular adventure. Spoiler alert: there is no other option.

She graces us with private and tender moments like being laid out on a doctor's office table, processing what for many is one of the most devastating sentences a woman can ever hear. I won't spoil what those words are. Just trust me. She graciously shares the rock-strewn path of how she ended up in that position in the doctor's office and how it came to transform her eventually. And then, like any great memoir, we begin down the healing road with her. Side by side. Travel becomes her healing ground as well as ours as we move through the narrative of her life and airplane rides.

We follow Melanie on a fourteen-day trek starting 7,600 miles away from home in Kathmandu, Nepal. We drive along the Colorado mountains as she learns to shed ill-fitting parental expectations and we watch the projector reel of memories like the first time she fell in love and the heartbreak that ensued when it was unrequited. It's certainly not Mission Impossible but I had to catch my breath as danger was evaded in a smoke-filled trip to Russia. In Melanie's version of a Choose Your Own Adventure book, we daydream with her as we stroll the streets of Paris and we share in her laughter during her "party phase" and the metaphorical hangover she learns to unpack and then release. We sit quietly beside her as she bears the abuse of toxic relationships and the vindication that follows. We dance in India celebrations of Diwali and sit in silence learning from yoga how to make space for repairing her soul. We kneel with her as she reconnects with her own spirituality and cheer as she says Yes to her life adventure soul mate. We share in the tears of empathy that well up in a Berlin cellar and those of anger from a DC elevator and all the while we may not have moved anywhere literally, we may still be sitting on our old velvet sofa with a cup of cold coffee, but we have gone everywhere with her, and with ourselves.

As the journey comes to a close- at least the journey in the book because no journey ever really comes to a close- we join in her call to action if we so choose and I pray we choose. I so pray we choose.

Incongruent is a tale of overcoming life's obstacles, regardless of how they present themselves. It's a lesson in grit, of authentic self-reflection, of healing. Within these pages are stories to inspire discovery within yourself. It took me down a path of emotions that felt as volatile as the mountain trek itself and I was made better for that coming alive. It's a book for adventure loving souls, for those longing to stay awake, for those feeling isolated because their life is so different from others or from their childhood dreams. I say that having your life look different others is cause for celebration and do does *Incongruent*. That doesn't give anything away in terms of plot; it simply nudges you in the butt with a slight kick that says you are doing just fine.

The book closes with a golden retriever named Molly who I live with in my imagination. Molly runs through the desert as she learns who she was meant to be and what she is truly capable of. Okay fine, maybe I don't live with Molly in my imagination. Maybe I am Molly. Maybe we all are.

With that last image of Molly galloping comes a wish to the reader that I also share. May we all discover who we are meant to be and what we are truly capable of. May we all learn to love our beautiful and unique life (maybe weird and wacky too), just as it is.

Jennifer Pastiloff,
Author, Speaker, Guru of Wacky and Weird

Incongruent

Prologue:
I'll Never Know

Altitude: Sea level
Travel Time: Infinite hypothetical miles
Soundtrack: Dog Days Are Over, Florence and the Machine

We need to get you scheduled for surgery as soon as possible."

His words echoed in the icy cold room causing an unconscious shiver to run over me. I sat alone in the standard-issue blue paper gown. The surge of emotions ran from fear to despair to relief. The journey to this moment had been nearly ten months in the making, and now I knew.

Near dawn on a warm, Florida, February morning, I discovered it. A chestnut-sized lump on the left side near my pelvic bone. For most of the following year, I alternated between rabbit hole internet digging and compartmentalizing to ignore.

I saw one doctor after another, taking test after test. I pleaded with doctor after doctor to keep trying new tests while results continued to be inconclusive. The experience gave me a doctorate in the American medical and insurance system. I began taking copies of every medical record and physically bringing them myself to new specialists. All the while, the months drew on, and the lump grew larger and more prominent.

By September, the lump was key lime-sized in my body and Godzilla-sized in my mind. I boarded a plane with my mom to Italy, and as I looked over at her deep into her iPad movie, I felt warm tears well in my eyes. I had yet to tell her anything, and I was determined not to until the trip was over. This was her first trip abroad and our longest mother-daughter excursion. I refused to allow her to be blanketed by the cloak of unknowing fear I was held under.

Then, after nearly ten months, here I was. A real diagnosis and all the realities of what was to come. A large, ambitiously growing fibroid, not cancerous but left untreated, dangerous, nonetheless.

"There is no guarantee, but we can try to save it."

I stared at the overly white walls as his words hung in the air for what felt like an eternity. I scanned the posters of smiling mothers and giggling babies before turning back to the ultrasound scan.

The fibroid, as most do, sits in the uterine wall. Though he wasn't referring to saving a baby. Only the organ that was designed to carry one. The organ that never got the chance in this body. A flood of emotion and thoughts and memories flashed before my eyes and welled up in my throat.

Two White Dresses

I married my college boyfriend despite a sea of red flag warnings. He was a ladies' man, a showboat constantly needing attention. The knot in my stomach grew larger each time I watched him buy a round of shots at the bar for strangers as our meager young-couple finances dwindled and debts rose. Unfortunately, everyone in my life saw this scenario coming and yet remained quiet.

Rows of books and boxes of colorful children's toys filled the Sunday school classroom where we waited. The lap of my hand-beaded, fluffy, white wedding dress was covered with a Hawaiian shirt as I ravaged a sandwich before the ceremony.

"Sooooo," my maid of honor and childhood best friend stood in front of me nervously fidgeting.

"What's up?" I muttered between bites.

"Listen, I am going to just say this . . . because, you know, my mom said it should be said to every bride. You know, just in case."

I looked up at her quizzically, suddenly aware that the rest of the wedding party had mysteriously left the room.

"If you are having any reservations, you can still call this off right now. I will go out there and send all those people home. You can just slip out the back."

I stared at her, unsure how to respond, feeling dozens of feelings at once. Could I? Could I really untangle this life I was committing to? What would she say to the 300 people in the church waiting for me? What would they say in response? What would my parents say? Our childhood intuitive connection has always revealed my deepest secrets. Did she sense the ugly tears of fear and despair I shed in the shower that morning? Did she know I sat on the shower floor, barely able to keep from throwing up, falsely assuring myself it was simply pre-wedding jitters?

I swallowed hard and pasted on a fake smile. "Nope, I am good," I lied. And just like that, the wheels of my life were forever altered.

By the end of our first year of marriage, our friends began to have children, and he began to inquire, with ever more persistence, when we would do the same. I was twenty-two years old, and although unable to articulate the reason, my gut told me this was not the path for me. His persistence soon turned to anger, and our future parent status became kindling for the fire that was soon a war within our home. But deep down I knew—he was unfit to be a father. Hell, he was barely fit to be a husband.

One night after a particularly volatile argument, I lay on our bedroom floor and stared up at the ceiling, the fan slowly turning round and round. Unable to stomach the realities of divorce, I decided to state a false claim that I did not want kids. That sacrifice, I rationalized, would save his ego and our marriage. We were divorced a year later. No surprise, I suppose, as a life can never grow roots when the soil is a lie.

As divorce papers were inked, someone else already held my attention. A chance meeting and an instant connection that left me reeling for years to come. My rational mind knew he was not available, but that wouldn't stop the butterflies that fluttered in my soul each time we crossed paths. And it seemed we both found reasons to cross paths often. Or was it only in my head?

During my separation, I moved out of my marital townhouse and into a tiny carriage house studio apartment. The moon would glisten off the lake outside my window as I lay awake at night dreaming of him. Followed ritualistically each morning with a sharp scolding of myself for thoughts so far from reality. A married man with a family, and yet, there was something in his eyes that I wanted to believe was telling me he was equally intrigued.

As the months drew on, he invited me to events around town under the guise of networking. I was more than happy to join if it meant we could share a few inside jokes and begin to build a repertoire of secrets only we understood. Our conversations became more vulnerable and more frequent. The ding of the message coming into my phone would bring a smile to my face before I even opened it. I was enamored and enthralled, ignoring the deafening warning sirens of my own naivete. I was the inevitable moth to a flame.

And then came the group text...a birth announcement. Pictures of him with his newborn son. Like a bucket of cold water, I was shocked back into reality from the fantasy world I had built in my mind. How ridiculous all those daydreams seemed in that moment. How childish I was to believe in some magical connection just because we shared deep thoughts over text. I may have started a life based on the farce of a fairy tale but who was I to believe anyone else was so foolish.

Over the next few months, I attempted to detach myself from these fanciful notions and refocus on my work and the doctorate degree I was completing. Until one political reception when I was introduced to the man who would become my second husband. I figured he would amount to a short-term fling, a distraction to help me move on. But he slowly began to win me over with his attention and doting. There were no magic butterflies or lingering, locked, eye gazes. There were no swooning daydreams or secret inside jokes. But surely those things were all delusions and this was real life, right?

He planned elaborate romantic excursions to the coast and wrote lavish love notes. I was blinded by the attention. I never imagined the danger it held. A road trip to Key West, a hammock, and a bottle of wine sealed our fate. But the dark clouds were already building.

The way he yelled when I got lost alone on a run and didn't come back to the hotel for two hours. The names he called me in anger when he was jealous at the way I looked at another at a football game. If only I had heeded the warning of nausea that washed over me regularly.

In far too short a time, we were moving in together. I knew it was a mistake, but he was so insistent. Only in hindsight could I see he was looking to secure our very unstable relationship with the trappings of domesticity.

Mere days after boxes were unpacked life took a staggering turn. Below the surface he held a dark side that when released changed swiftly to rage, anger, and manipulation. My reaction to this side of him went from shock to fear to denial very early on.

The clock read 6:02 p.m. when I walked through the door of the temporary rental we were living in while house hunting. The energy I met was angry and oppressive.

"Where have you been? Why weren't you home earlier?" The words hurled with an accusatory and sharp yell.

A lump formed in my stomach that would not truly release for the next three years. "I went to the post office," I stammered, shocked by the implication. "There was a line."

He slammed down the dinner plate in his hand. I stared helplessly at the shards of broken porcelain on the floor as a feeling I only understood later flooded my soul—foreboding.

And so it began. The whiplash of a roller coaster ride filled with peaks of his adoration plunging sharply and without warning into deep valleys of manipulation and emotional abuse.

With each passing day the insults got worse, the threats more dangerous, and the emotional scars more severe. And yet rather than retreat from him, I clung tighter. Perhaps I was too proud to admit to anyone the huge mistake I had made. Perhaps I was too ashamed to look at myself in the mirror. Life became a delicate walk on eggshells, carefully navigating potential angry bursts.

Michelle Jewsbury describes this kind of love in her book, *But I Love Him:*

> *Falling in love and being fearful are a lot alike. They both give you that anxious feeling of butterflies in your stomach, a sense of excitement, and a general unease physically and mentally. It is easy to confuse love with fear. I thought I was in love. Looking back, I realized I was scared for reasons yet to be known.*

My mind flashes back to an Atlanta hotel room in 2008. I am standing at the 24th floor window overlooking the city, holding my Blackberry away from my ear. By then he was my husband, and he was yelling loudly enough to echo across the room, threatening to kick me out of our home by placing my belongings in the front yard. It was a definitive moment that began my escape. I wasn't a perfect wife, but the gaslighting was not going to make me one either.

"If this is how you would like to treat me while I am away on a work trip, then I suppose I can purchase new things. I need to go now. I will see you in two days when I return." And I hung up.

But why did I stay? Where was that voice of strength that brought me out of my first marriage? Why was I vowing to double down to make this work, however dysfunctional? Because it was allegedly what was real? Or perhaps because of *them.*

Along with this man came two amazing humans. At five and two years old, they were full of love and light. I was instantly smitten the day I met them. Just hearing them call for my attention provided a love bubble rush like none other. "Ms. Melanie, will you read that to me again?" "Ms. Melanie, will you play Legos with me?" They have a fabulous mom who always remained the core of stability and love for them. But, as only children can, they held enough love for me as well. And I loved them. I loved them in a way I never knew was possible. Loved them so deeply I could not imagine a life without them. Could not imagine the idea of not being their stepmom at their baseball games and dance recitals, graduations and weddings.

Knowing how to stepparent, especially in a tumultuous relationship, is a hero's feat. I worked very intentionally to never give an impression I was a replacement for even a hint of their real parents. Rather, I tried only to add meaning as a third source of love. But best intentions can go awry, and we all make missteps. My patience would be frazzled by the volatility between their father and I, leaving less for them than they deserved. My frustration at the financial burdens I was carrying after their father lost his job would taint my desire to splurge on family activities the way I wanted to. My fatigue at battling the constant eggshell vigilance left me tired and not as energetic as I desired to be with them.

A few months in, I took to venting to friends who offered first advice and then warning and concern. All of which I ignored despite acknowledging their accuracy. When the outbursts became more violent and more public and my excuses began to be ignored, I retreated from friends and family to protect the secret we held within our relationship. However, their words continued to plead with me to find my lost self.

> *I think you both tell me half-truths, you both want to do the right thing, but you're both fucking idiots! I am going to stop talking to both of you until you each take seriously how important reality is. I loved you both when you were not insane! I don't even like either of you when you're like this. My relationship with you guys is low priority for each of you, but it is exhausting for me. You guys go and keep this bullshit up and someone*

> *will get hurt and someone will go to prison. But it is on you guys—no one else! You both have a ton of friends that want to help—but you keep feeding us bullshit. I'll be here when you guys come out on the other side. I just hope you each make it in one piece.*

Friend's Text

I was unwilling to listen. Unwilling to get help for myself or get out. I brushed them off as just not understanding the bond we had. However, deep down I knew there was no bond, only lies. Before long, I was soothing myself in the false narrative of being a helpless victim. The truth was much harder to stomach.

> *You are a brilliant, beautiful, successful woman—act like one! Move on, take grown-up steps to put all of this behind you. Otherwise, you could lose it all. It is one thing to be sad and mourn a loss; it is another thing to obsess and allow it to destroy you. Fix it!*

Friend's Text

In my own mind I began to block out the negative and focus only on the good times, no matter how few and far between. I would stare at myself in the mirror in disbelief. I am an educated, ambitious woman from a good family—things like this don't happen to people like me. And yet I knew that was not true, and I could no longer avoid the truth.

Years later, a simple victim's advocate pamphlet would illuminate this as a pattern of behavior so textbook in its replicability, my academic mind would break into hysterics. But in the moment, there was no laughter to be had. There was only survival. And in this survival, I nearly lost myself.

Surviving a volatile relationship requires a toolbox of reactionary defense mechanisms. None of them represent our highest selves. At least not for me. It took me mere weeks to stock my toolkit with quiet compliance and alcohol-infused memory erasers.

The real tools I was gathering were far darker. A growing sense of resentment evolved into my own sharp tongue. I honed my ability to spit slights as cutting as those I dodged. As my outward anger grew more public, inwardly I spiraled into a deeper and deeper hole of despair. Friends drifted away, unable to continue offering advice to be ignored. Unwilling to watch the impending train wreck ahead.

Until, at last, it was done.

The tiles on our bathroom floor were chilly despite the heat of the afternoon sun through the window. I sat motionless, knees hugged in tight, staring at myself in the floor length mirror. *How did I let this happen?* was my only thought; yet it was running through my mind on continuous repeat.

Although separated, we had continued to see each other as "friends," another way he had convinced me to stay intertwined. Another way to give up my own control and power to heal and move on. On that previous night, we met for wings and beer. A mutual friend, one of the only ones still willing, joined us. The night began without incident, talking football and catching up. Or so I perceived. Weeks later our friend would illustrate to me the ping-pong of slights we had passive-aggressively hurled all evening. A pattern so habitual it was indiscernible in the moment.

As he entertained us with a story about his daughter's go-kart reluctance, I made a snarky joke about his lack of understanding her feminine preferences. Out of nowhere, he erupted. A red rage filled his eyes as he yelled in my face, and then the world went black as my head hit the tile floor, and the stool I was sitting on crashed down next to me. I awoke a few moments later, dazed as much from the sharp reality of the public physical act of violence as from the concussion it left in its wake. Our friend snuck out quietly as the police and ambulance were called. My estranged husband left as well, leaving me all alone to sit in my shame and disbelief.

The next morning as I stepped out of the shower, I read the text. At the forceful urging of the restaurant, I had filed a formal report of the incident with the police who had arrived on scene. In order to avoid a mandatory hospital visit, I was careful to mention only a sore tailbone in the police report and not the concussion making me blurry-eyed and nauseous. Refusing the ambulance or even a hospital visit, they drove me home before heading straight to his house where he was promptly arrested…in the middle of the night, with his kids sleeping in the next room. I felt simultaneously horrified and vindicated. And overwhelmingly nauseous.

I slid down the wall to the bathroom floor where I stayed for hours. Every scene of our short relationship rotated through my mind. There were the sins we both shared—the insults, the jealousy, the frenetic text messages, the fierce battles fueled by anger, alcohol, and resentment. And there were the sins that only he bore—the threats of violence, the broken laptop, the holes punched in the door and the wall, my broken finger, my closet strewn out on the lawn. All of it rapidly destroying our livelihoods, our relationships, and our lives.

I'm not crying because of you; you're not worth it. I am crying because my delusion of who you were was shattered by the truth of who you are.

Steve Maraboli

The day the divorce was final, my friends cheered and toasted, but for me it was just another exercise for my carefully honed false smile. Inside I was devastated. That night I wandered through my now-empty house hearing the lost sounds of children's laughter and his yelling all mixed in my head. I slept on the floor of the living room that night, looking out at the Capital and the moon. I was grieving—not for him or our marriage, but for them. I grieved for the part of me that died that day, the part of me that somehow knew this was the closest I would get to motherhood. Looking back, I will always wish I had done better, and yet I will always know I did the best I could. I was a twenty-something new stepparent, in an unstable relationship, giving as much love as I could muster.

How had I let this happen? It's a question that would take me years to really understand. But eventually, it would become clear. I chose to disengage from my own intellect and more importantly my own gut. I chose to compartmentalize. To believe each fleeting moment of beauty would not be stolen yet again by the dark. And I chose to become a chameleon. I abandoned my own values of love and calm and rationality. I took up the sword and shield in anger and became the same bitter, warring faction I was fighting against. I was far from a victim. Perhaps there was a moment that was true. But by the end, I was a willing participant in the bloody battle. A battle that would take years to rise above. Years of continuing to carry the heavy burden of resentment softened by the crutch of alcohol.

No matter how hard it is, you have to get through it. You have to get out. It's worth it. If you are living in fear or dread of another person, you have to make a plan to get out of it. If you find yourself in an unhappy relationship, do everything you can to leave. I stayed too long, hoping that other people would change or that the situation would change. But nothing changed until I made a change.

Maye Musk,
A Woman Makes a Plan, pg. 74

The Empty Rocking Chair

Over the next decade, slowly and imperfectly, I came back to life. Friends returned, as did my own spirituality and self-worth. I grew, or perhaps just rekindled, my own sense of wanderlust as I explored more than thirty U.S. cities and forty countries. I grew my career, tended my nest egg, and planted seeds of my bigger dreams. And I even had a few fleeting love affairs along the way. My ex-husband also healed after our split in his own way; growing his career and finding a lifelong love that suited him much better than I ever could. As unlikely as it was, something about both of us thriving offered a sense of closure.

I thought often about kids and my lack thereof. It is nearly impossible in your thirties not to, as everyone your age is either caring for them or pining for them. I knew I had traded my most formative childbearing years to an unhealthy relationship and the healing thereafter. These thoughts held an occasional tinge of regret, which I quickly squashed with intentional gratitude for the life I had built in its stead.

However, all alone on that doctor's table, this was my reality now. I would never know what my babies would look like. I look identical to my mother. Would they have as well or taken more from their father? I would never know that infamous smell of my infant's head that mothers and grandmothers are drawn to like a drug. I would never know if I'd decorate a baby's room in blue, my favorite color, or yellow like my own Winnie-the-Pooh childhood room. I would never rock a baby to sleep in the wooden rocking chair that held two generations of cooing babies in my family.

One month later, I awoke in a hospital recovery room. My hand immediately went to my abdomen where four, tiny, raised scars were all that remained of the physical part of me that could once carry a life.

As I lay ruminating on this, a stark realization crept over me. I looked at my life up to that point and realized I had allowed far too many miles to pass my window before I was brave enough to admit I was lost. There were flashy road signs and helpful highway patrolmen along the way, but no one can give you directions to places they have never been. For me, I always felt lost, no matter how trusted the source, and I never understood why. So, I simply kept running. Pushing through life with a forced ferocity. Pretending that "you only live once" was an excuse to live carelessly. Bowing to societal norms, fearing the consequences of walking an individualized path, I kept life as close to on the rails as I could. And felt extreme shame when I failed. Until the day I woke up.

Questions Left Unanswered

Where would my life have gone if I had allowed the escape of a runaway bride all those years earlier? Enduring the fallout would have created immediate strength that instead took many years to cultivate. Would that strength have fine-tuned my ability to see truth from delusion? Would that ability have kept me from the roller coaster of my second marriage? Avoiding both would have altered my financial life indefinitely. Where would I have allowed that financial freedom to take me? Who would I have met? Who would I have become? Would I have been a mom?

I am often fraught with guilt for choosing partners so poorly equipped and squandering the time my body might have been healthy enough to carry a child. But other times, I deeply believe the universe always held a different path for me. Either way, I will never know. But one thing is certain, it is now more important than ever to close old wounds and heal old scars.

Then on this day, in one revelatory moment, I stopped. I got quiet enough to hear the Waze of my inner voice. Being childless meant walking a path that differed from other women. It also meant a blur of complicated emotions to traverse. There were the dark paths. I felt alone, different, and left out of the shared community of mothers, unable to relate to the triumphs and challenges of child rearing. I felt ostracized, shamed, and misunderstood by the child-centric society we live in, where motherhood is often hailed as a woman's greatest accomplishment. I felt guilt and regret for not giving the joy of a grandchild to my parents. I felt the fear of being completely alone in my elder and most vulnerable years.

But then there were all the emotions of light and hope. Being childless allows a freedom that no mother can ever experience. A complete uncaging from societal expectations; unencumbered to live the most enlightened and robust life of my choosing. A feeling of empowerment to live a life of pure curiosity as consequences of failure have so little impact without a child in tow. Free to be thoughtful and introspective or wild and outlandish without hesitation.

And then there were the most complicated of emotions. There is an unexplained sense of relief, as if I had narrowly escaped a treacherous path not meant for me. Relief that I can live this unencumbered life, not subject to the cloak of motherhood that simply doesn't seem to fit properly for me.

Instead, I felt a sense of enhanced purpose. Obituaries highlight all of those left behind by the dead. What would be left to say in mine? Without a child would the end of my life leave me simply undervalued or completely unseen by the world? Suddenly I was more resolute than ever about legacy building. I felt relentless to use my short time on earth more wisely. To drink in every drop of fun and let go of everything else. I wrestled with the feeling I had something to prove. To show the world, or perhaps just myself, that I matter, that I can make an impact without being a parent.

> *A childless friend once said to me, I will never regret not having children. What I regret is that I live in a world where in spite of everything that decision is still not quite okay.*
>
> Pam Houston, "The Trouble with Having it All",
> Selfish, Shallow, and Self-Absorbed: Sixteen Writers on the
> Decision Not to Have Kids , *pg. 171*

There is no white picket fence and 2.5 children in my future. There would be no family traditions to pass on. No hoping for the next generation to do more, be more. There is only now, only this life. From here on, it is only me. Whatever I wanted to give to this world had to come from me. Every choice I made from here on would define the legacy I left behind. And boy, did that legacy need work!

The Path to the Mountain

The below freezing temperatures are no match for our glowing radiance. Standing ten feet above the ground on the famously spray-painted rock, we raise our arms in triumph. Here we stand, elated, nearly 18,000 feet above sea level, at Everest Base Camp. Attempting to memorize the scene below, I beg my soul to permanently imprint this feeling on my psyche.

In *Bird by Bird*, Ann Lamott tells a story of her tonsillectomy nurse instructing her to chew gum as a form of pain relief. The nurse explained that when we have a wound in the body, the muscles around it cramp to protect it, and the only way to relax them is through use and motion. Lamott goes on to compare this physical reaction of the body to the same reaction in our psychic muscles.

> *They cramp around our wounds—the pain from our childhood, the losses and disappointment of adulthood, the humiliations suffered in both—to keep us from getting hurt in the same place again.*

The reasons for making this trek differ widely. Some revel in the adventure. Some cross an item off their bucket list. Some add content to their Instagram feed. And some, like me, need to experience the discomfort to be reminded what being alive feels like. I needed to traverse the literal and metaphorical trail to uncramp the muscles around life's wounds.

For a while I began calling this journey of self-discovery "Becoming Congruent." I thought I needed to realign my life to some version of congruence to what was acceptable, normalized. And then one day I realized I was rolling a boulder up a mountain. What I really needed was to go inside myself. To excavate my attic, open all the boxes, blow off all the dust, and really see myself for who I was. Only then could I learn to love all of those misshapen pieces. Only then could I define a life where those pieces come together to form a beautiful piece of oddly shaped art to give to the world. I needed to love my life *because* it is incongruent with the norm.

Doing this work took years. Years in the dark followed by a cold examination table realization. I spent years healing, living, becoming who I truly wanted to be and will continue the work for the rest of my life.

> *The grief she experienced and thought she would never overcome has allowed her to grow, as she observes how grief transforms the devastation of loss into an unsentimental ability to face reality, to accept life on its terms, not on ours.*

Jody Day, 2017 TEDx talk,
The Lost Tribe of Childless Women

Illustrated by my sixteen-day expedition through Nepal, this book is both the realities of the physical trek and a treasure trove of life lessons recounted along the way. It is my own figurative trek into the looking glass of my soul. As I placed one foot in front of the other, I reflected on the people, places, and experiences that made me the person I am. Gratitude for the good, the bad, and even the ugly that led me to this point in time. Gratitude for my incongruent life and the train of happiness that I simply cannot escape.

Chapter 1:
The Flight East

Altitude: 43,000ft
Travel Time: 7,733 miles; Flight time seventeen hours
Soundtrack: Fly Away, Tones and I

Dressed in my favorite gray travel pants and accompanied by my love and two best friends, I boarded a plane in Orlando, Florida, heading east to Nepal. The excitement was palpable as we drank airport margaritas and predicted what would lie ahead. How hard would the trek be? How cold would the temperatures dip? Did we pack everything we should? Did we pack too much?

At eight days up the mountain, six days down and a few days of sea level recuperation, it was the longest hiking journey any of us had ever attempted, at least for pleasure. Randy, whose Army Ranger training and multiple combat tours had given ample opportunity to endure the elements, was perhaps the only one with intimate knowledge of what was ahead.

The Emirates Airline Boeing 777 sat ten seats across; however, we secured the odd side aisle with only two seats together. Our own little cubby of coziness. As we settled into our seats, I watched the other passengers as they boarded: American tourists, Middle Eastern businessmen, families with small children in tow. I pondered each of their stories and reasons for the journey.

As the plane ascended into the blue sky, I watched the ground disappear below out the airplane window. So many of my most inspired and impactful moments of life have happened while looking out an airplane window.

My connection to travel is nothing short of spiritual, holding the most powerful of life's lessons. It began as a child. Whether it was the quick spring weekend escapes, the traditional fall football trips, or the six-week-at-a-time summer extravaganzas, we loaded into an RV to travel the country in search of adventure. While my parents thought they were teaching me a little about geography and this great country of ours, these memorable vacations would turn out to be the concrete foundations of my soul.

Postcards from A Child

Standing at the rail overlooking the largest waterfall in the world is breathtaking at any age. Yet at twelve, it was not the power of the water that drew my attention, it was the endless list of people who had dared with their lives to conquer this great body of water.

Annie Taylor is credited as the first person to ever defeat the falls in a wooden barrel in 1901. Her name is forever etched in my memory. It would seem the lesson here is to be unafraid of risk and go after your dreams, yet ironically Annie never received praise for her efforts and died years later while living in poverty. For Annie and the many that followed, the risk did not guarantee the reward. So, I wrestled through life wondering when and if the risk is worth the reward, and how will I know? How do I cultivate a life where I don't fear risk while still protecting myself? Until the day I realized that I was wrestling with the wrong question. It isn't about risk versus reward—it is about risk versus regret. And in that moment, I made a promise to myself. If there is something in life that I wake up thinking of and go to bed at night dreaming about then it is worth the risk. And yet I would break this promise to myself many times.

There is no better way to understand the sheer majesty of the Grand Canyon than from a raft navigating its way through the treacherous, whitecapped waters of the Colorado River. The trip was six hours long despite feeling like fifteen minutes. As the youngest and lightest on the raft, I was seated at the very back as we prepared to brave the rapids. Much of the trip was spent craning my neck to see the varied colors of yellow, red, and orange that graced the sides of the seemingly endless canyon. Yet just when you gazed off too long the river reminded you of its power.

One such reminder came about two hours into the trip when a sudden dip over a not-so-small waterfall sent me flying off the back of the raft. There are only three things I remember about this incident. One, the shock of the frigid water as it hit my face. Two, the sound of my mother's scream, and three, the feel of my father's hand grasping my arm and knowing he would never let me go. There is nothing like Mother Nature to remind you that you aren't invincible, and there is nothing like the strong hand of a father to remind you that sometimes you have to reach out and let someone save you.

Tijuana, Mexico, in the mid-1980s was a textbook view of all things Mexico—dry and dusty with bustling markets filled with handmade Mexican artifacts that leave an eight-year-old wide-eyed. There were no resorts or high rises to be seen. No high-priced shops or swanky bars and restaurants to pass through. We traveled by charter bus along with forty strangers through customs and into the city. We were to see a bullfight, but first, I convinced my father I could not possibly live without those larger-than-life paper flowers from the market.

"Do not get them wet," said the man in broken English.

With my bouquet in hand, I paraded into the coliseum on cloud nine. The show of bulls and dancers with their colorful ribbons and capes was jaw dropping until…. No one warned me they would kill the bull in the end. My heart ached for that strange creature and his untimely death. And another of life's more difficult lessons was acquired. I watched as my teardrops rolled down my cheeks onto those beautiful paper flowers leaving permanent spots and cried even harder at the thought of their ruin. To my surprise, once dry, the flowers were still beautiful and even more meaningful with their dotted texture. It was years later when I realized the significance of this moment. Life's disappointments will nearly always come at you with no warning and will leave permanent reminders on your soul. Yet moving forward, it is those individual reminders that make us more beautiful.

There is a field in northern New Jersey where RVs park. With nary a building in sight, one would never know you were only a short drive to the greatest city in our country. We parked overnight in preparation for braving the big city the next day. The evening was pleasant, and we pulled chairs up around a small radio to enjoy the late summer sunset.

I had a friend on this trip, the granddaughter of our travel mates. Together over a month by now, we knew every song on the radio and could finish each other's thoughts. This night was no exception. At first the adults tried to calm us down; "its nearing bedtime," they said. "You need to get baths." But eventually admitting defeat, they just let us wear ourselves out. We sang and danced into the late hours of the night. We laughed until our sides hurt. We lay on the ground and drew pictures in the stars. We watched our parents and grandparents dance and smile and remember why they still loved each other. We had traveled thousands of miles and seen all the attractions that money could buy. And yet, this night in a New Jersey field would be the memory I cherish most. I think of this night often when I find myself caught in the routines of life. Perhaps living on a child's timeline, every once in a while, can be good for all our souls.

Beyond the summers, the RV was part of a family tradition that began long before I was born and continued long after. Nearly every fall Friday, sharply at 3:00 p.m., my mother and I arrived home from school to find my father and the RV waiting in the driveway ready to depart. It was a football weekend, and we were headed to my mother's alma mater. It was a short, four-hour drive interrupted only by the traditional stop in Montgomery for dinner.

As we pulled off the interstate and made our way to campus, the familiar painted paw prints directed our path. The much anticipated moment of opening the door and smelling the fall air was something I never tired of. These weekends were full of traditions from the Friday night pep rallies to Saturday afternoon Tiger Walks, from Toomer's Corner lemonade to face painting at Tiger Rags. What emerged from these weekends, beyond my love of football, was a sense of community that I have yet to ever experience again. Our family was part of a unique group of longtime season ticket holders that literally spent decades together one weekend at a time. During most of the year, they were parents of future Heisman winners, Trustees of the Board, well-known businessmen, influential politicians, teachers, policemen, and plumbers. But every football weekend they were simply Tiger fans.

We were a part of a second family that was a literal representation of a village that raises a child. The bonds were much deeper than simple pleasantries or acknowledgments by name; it was a genuine smile that welcomed you "home." The adults made meals, played cards, and enjoyed the campfires, while the kids played touch football, ran races, and climbed trees. We celebrated team victories and bemoaned defeats. We knew each other's birthdays and anniversaries. We threw parties when couples were married or babies were born and grieved and comforted when someone was lost. This community taught me that the definition of family is wide reaching. Family can mean anywhere that hearts and memories collide. For when you care enough, a few weekends a year can be all you need.

There were a few years we added a winter excursion to our annual adventures. Over these years, we skied our way from the soft powder snow of Park City, Utah, to the icy slopes of Crested Butte, Colorado. As a Florida beach girl, I was never truly at home on the slopes, but the feeling of the brisk mountain air rushing over me was as invigorating as any I have ever felt. Each trip I would put my courage to the test and worked to push a little farther and go a little faster. However, despite my best efforts, caution always outweighed my tolerance for risk. Until the day I landed on the lift next to a talkative boy my age.

As we chatted away about where we were from and how long we were staying, I obliviously missed my jump spot for the blue slope, and before I knew it, only a black diamond lay between me and the comfort of the lodge. My new friend leaped confidently and was thirty yards ahead before turning to inquire what was holding me up. I certainly wasn't going to admit my inexperience, much less my sheer fright, so with much trepidation, I smiled and followed. To my great surprise, I zipped down the steep inclines with effortless glee. Even tackling the moguls, certainly in comical form, simply laughing at myself along the way.

As we landed safely at the bottom of the mountain, I looked back upon my accomplishment with a sense of quiet pride that would resonate with me for years to come. What joy I had missed out on by being so cautious and fearful. Where else in life have I let my own fears rob me of potential joy? To this day, I push hard on myself to choose laughter over fear.

And then there was the summer we traded the RV adventure for plane tickets to the Hawaiian Islands. Greeted with leis at the airport, we were immediately immersed in this cultural wonderland, exploring island after island, learning their customs, and enjoying their cuisine. I found my own disdain for poi and a love of black sand beaches. Yet among the leis and luaus, snorkeling and exploring, this tropical paradise had unexpected aspects of solemn reflection and introspective refinement. We climbed a volcanic summit to witness the steam as the lava flow slowly seeped from a hole worn in the side of the mountain into the ocean. As we made our way closer, the once paved road became covered in the dried remains of the last lava flow. The hard black bubbles were frozen in time. Signs pointed the way to follow a path where the lava was safe to traverse yet warned of the increasing heat that could damage the soles of your shoes. The danger signs got larger and more prominent as you moved closer and closer to the summit but none stopped you from reaching the much anticipated view of live lava flow.

In recapping this experience, it made me long for those same signs to direct my path in life. What reassurance it would be to see the looming caution signs when you are about to misstep. What encouragement it would be to never worry you had gone too far. And what comfort to be warned when to anticipate damaging heat ahead. How would life be different if you could read the signs of life as easily as the signs of lava?

And so, these lessons of risk taking, vulnerability, growing from hurt, slowing down for life, being stronger than fear, and listening for the signs of life are among the many things I thank my parents for providing me and hold close to my heart. True life lessons were hidden within those faded postcards of the many destinations of my childhood and thus began my love for travel.

Rice Paper Lanterns

As an adult, travel primarily revolved around work conferences and visiting of friends and family. By my thirtieth birthday, I was twice divorced and happily single. Finally regaining my own sense of self, I found actual comfort in days spent solo, with no agenda but my own. When a work conference in Portland, Oregon, a destination unknown for me, presented itself, I took advantage of this newfound freedom and booked an additional week of solo travel.

Portland International Airport baggage claim was chilly and crowded. Minutes turned into more than an hour as we stood waiting for the buzzing red light of the conveyor belt. An unassuming man, ten years my senior or more, in a University of Kentucky sweatshirt began making small talk: Kentucky basketball, airline turbulence, Portland weather. Despite his southern accent, he is a local to Portland and assures me this time delay is an anomaly. I share my trip's dual purpose and my personal intention on solo adventure. He offers tips from restaurants to sightseeing. As the conveyor belt finally begins moving, he offers an unexpected invitation. He and a group of friends will be touring local vineyards the following day if I want to join.

"No pressure," he says handing me his business card. "My girlfriend will also be there." I hesitantly take it, thank him, and make my way to the taxi stand.

That night in the hotel, I hold his card in my hands as I ponder the decision to reach out. Is this a gift from the travel gods or something I should be wary of? With a little apprehension but a greater sense of YOLO, I send an email accepting the invitation. After a few moments, I hear the ping of a reply message. With surprise in his tone, he sends over logistics for the following morning.

At ten minutes after eight the next morning, a green Honda pulled up to the front of my hotel to pick me up. A pretty brunette with an unassuming and casual demeanor introduces herself as Jessie, a friend of Kentucky's. Instantly, my anxiety fades. As we make the half hour drive, we are astonished to learn that first, we both attended grad school at Florida State, next, we both went to the same elementary school, and finally, we shared the same third grade teacher. The odds of this encounter are so rare they seem like a farce.

Whether you call it a coincidence, a God wink, or a sign from the Universe, I knew in that moment on the car ride that this day and this trip would come to represent something important in my life.

We arrived at a large, peach-colored, three-story house on a hill. Kentucky greeted us warmly, and the small group began to gather in his living room for introductions and small talk.

A few moments later, his girlfriend, a tall, stunning, blonde, younger than me, arrived home from her shift as a nurse at the hospital. The look on her face said everything. She had no idea who I was, why I was there, and wasn't thrilled to find out. Immediately, Kentucky swooped in to explain, and within moments we were all climbing into a black suburban to begin the tour.

Wine tours in northern Oregon feel nothing like their California counterpart. The landscape of old farmhouses and tractors provide a rustic non-pretentious backdrop. We visited four vineyards, each more interesting than the last. At our final stop, near dusk, we sipped by an outdoor firepit with the owners, Kentucky's friends.

Over the crackle of the fire, we shared stories—none of them particularly noteworthy, but all of them ending in laughter. We capped off the evening back at Kentucky's home over a feast of fresh salmon and vegetables on his grille. Belly full, I bid my goodbyes and expressed my gratitude before Jessie drove me back to my hotel.

Over the next week, I remained open to whatever came forth, and the unusual experiences continued. I rode the trolley, watched old men play chess in the park, photographed the dragons in Chinatown, and had a drink in the tallest building overlooking the city at sunset. I rented a car for a day and drove the circle around Mount Hood, stopping to walk in a sunflower field, see a glassblowing demonstration, and hike Multnomah Falls. I met up with Jessie once more to wander through the Portland International Rose Test Garden.

One afternoon while shopping in the Pearl District, I stopped to photograph a metal horse painted red and adorned with red and yellow flowers. As I turned, I noticed a rice paper lamp store hidden in the half basement of a clothing boutique. The owner, a small man of Asian descent, caught my intense curiosity of a particular hanging lamp and asked if I was interested in learning how they make them. Three hours later, I was in the store's back room, elbow deep in rice paper and glue, learning the beautiful ancient art with his wife. They sent me home with supplies to remake that hanging lamp on my own.

I spent my final night in Portland at a hilltop five-star restaurant, dining on a four-course meal, sipping a bottle of Perrier and a glass of champagne. All things that felt both luxurious and foreign. Unlike other solo meals, I left my phone in my purse and was simply present. I tasted every drop of garlic and butter on the escargot and every touch of wood plank char on the salmon. I savored the bubbles in my champagne and the sweet tang of the strawberry on my chocolate torte. I thought only of that moment and a few reflections of the week.

I had taken the trolley to dinner, but it was too late to take it back. There were no Ubers to be found—as they were only recently open in Portland—so after a half hour of waiting on a traditional taxi, I began the slow walk back downtown to the hotel.

As I turned the corner entering the warehouse district, I was immediately immersed in a jovial crowd. Before long I saw the near miles of tents and dozens of galleries. I had stumbled into the arts district, and like every other piece of magic in this trip, it was festival night. Galleries in this part of town are set up high in old shipping bays, and on festival nights they poured wine, played music, and stayed open well into the night. Art students and other local artists are encouraged to set up tents or displays on the ground level below.

I wandered through the galleries and booths for hours. I asked each of the students and local artists for their stories and casually eavesdropped on the patron purchases at the high-end galleries. Shoes in hand, I left that night with a single pair of hand-cut, metal earrings, a pair of blistered feet, and an ever-deepening love of art and festivals.

This adventure would prove to be the first of many solo trips. Nearly thirty cities around the US would follow, each bringing their own unique pleasure but none holding the magic of the first. Baseball stadium tours, concerts in unique venues, random insomnia plane bookings—there were so many reasons to travel and nearly none to dissuade. With each journey, the life lessons mounted, and the bravery compounded.

And while solo travel gave me independence, group travel opened my eyes to more of the human experience. In the years to follow, I would join groups of strangers that became friends to explore the world. Groups of all sizes, nationalities, and intentions. Crossing the globe, each experience would add its own life lesson to take away and preserve. People who would remain lifelong friends, and some I would never see again.

Sadly, I never made that paper lantern. Despite my meticulous lessons, the rice paper sat for many years before becoming fancy holiday wrapping paper. Like so many of my adventures over the years, I boarded a plane and left it all behind. Quickly turning to the next thing, I just kept running.

I close the airplane window shade and then my eyes, trying to place the exact feeling in my stomach. A strange mix of anticipatory butterflies and rear-facing longing.

> *Nothing feels better than going home, and nothing*
> *feels better than leaving home—the bittersweet curse.*
>
> Josh Homme, Queens of the Stone Age front man, said to
> Anthony Bourdain in an episode of "No Reservations" 2011.

How does one know the difference between experiencing life and chasing after the illusion of an oasis? And even if you know, are both OK? For tonight, I am just here to fly away.

Chapter 2:
Dubai Layover

Altitude: Sea level
Travel Time: Eighteen-hour layover
Soundtrack: Daydream, Lily Meola

The wheels of our Boeing 777 touched down with remarkable softness. After a little over fourteen hours, we have arrived in the Vegas of the Middle East. On a journey my parents could not even imagine, our eighteen-hour layover allows time to briefly explore Dubai. This will be my second Dubai experience in less than a year.

Dubai, the largest city in the United Arab Emirates, is located on the southeast coast of the Persian Gulf, in the Arabian Desert, and is the capital of the Emirate of Dubai, one of the seven emirates that make up the country. Dubai is a modern marvel. Not only does it have a thriving and sophisticated banking system but its pro-business policy and legal structure welcomes businesses from across the globe. Dubai also hosts a thriving global tourist market with luxury shopping, ultramodern architecture, and lively nightlife.

My first Dubai encounter, six months earlier, was a gifted trip from Randy. Contracted to run the Afghanistan unit for his company only a few months after we met, he promised to meet me halfway through his deployment for a weekend in Dubai. Our short time together there was pure bliss. Moonlit dinner cruises, awestruck shopping excursions, and guided bus tours so mundane we each took turns napping. We explored with veracity, embarking on the complete tourist experience.

And now here we stood again. The same airport, in the same city, on a completely different journey.

Exiting the expansive airport, the hot desert air is akin to a smack in the face. Our Lyft vehicles, high-end Mercedes, speak volumes to the type of wealth found in this city. We head toward The Dubai Mall. As the endless skyscrapers and ultramodern scenery passes by my window, I debate if the wealth of this city or its safety is more difficult to fathom. As a middle-class American, it is difficult to comprehend the freedom that much wealth would allow. Generations of oil assets and legacies of family wealth are on full display throughout the city's culture. I have no idea what a life of this magnitude would entail.

We step inside The Dubai Mall desert oasis and are met with a rush of air conditioning and frenetic energy. The mall holds more than five million square feet of retail space, primarily luxury brands from Europe including Gucci, Prada, Fendi, and Louis Vuitton, and on this day is filled with hundreds of shoppers. As the group winds its way through the endless hallways, slowly window shopping, I am relishing the diversity of the people. From young European lovers dressed in fashionable, trendy attire to traditional, middle eastern families, wives in full burkas with multiple kids and a non-Muslim nanny in tow. There were suited businessmen engaging in intense conversation and groups of older men or women sipping coffee with seemingly nowhere to be.

Around the corner is a pinnacle of beauty. In the center of the mall is the Dubai Aquarium with its 2.6 million gallon main tank on display, free to all mall visitors. On my first trip, I had one day alone after Randy left. I stood in front of the massive glass tank for what seemed like an eternity. Mesmerized by the effortless motion of the sharks, stingrays, and colorful schools as they danced in an eternal water ballet.

Just outside the aquarium is a Turkish restaurant with an appealing menu. We opt for the outdoor patio of colorful umbrellas and immediately order. Within moments, intricately carved silver trays of frothy Turkish coffee arrive alongside traditional accoutrements of water and sugar cubes. We graciously accept the lesson on the proper way to consume and partake as we await our feast. At long last, crescent-shaped trays filled with hearty baba ghanouj, silky smooth hummus, tangy mint and garlic yogurt, earthy tahini, and crisp tzatziki accompanied by baskets of freshly baked flatbreads. With each bite the conversation becomes more and more inaudible leaving only the sounds of our gluttonous delight.

As I look around the table, I am completely overcome with emotion. How is it I came to be in this place, with these souls, on this journey? Intrinsically I know it was not one choice but a series of deepening convictions to live the fullest human experience life allows. I close my eyes and raise a quiet prayer of gratitude, glad no one notices the dampness in my eyes.

Once fully satiated, our group calls a series of Lyfts and head toward the most iconic structure in all of Dubai, if not the world—the Burj Khalifa.

As we pass the endless string of large white mosques, I hear the distinct sound of the call to prayer, and my stomach does a small flip. Like most Americans, I share an innate fear of the Middle East. After terrorist attacks on 9/11 and two decades of war in Iraq and Afghanistan, our view of the entire region has been skewed to violence, poverty, and suffering. It is human nature to generalize things we do not understand. As it relates to the Middle East, we conflate regionality with religion, fueling our fear of all symbols of the Muslim faith. In my heart, I know this correlation is misaligned, but my internalized fight-or-flight response picks up its head for a split second anyhow.

In truth, I hold a unique fascination with the Muslim prayer ritual. The ritual, in its simplest form, strikes me as a beautiful way to hold space for planned moments of reconnection throughout our day. A purposeful deep breath and calming outreach to our personal spiritual beliefs. I find it disheartening that extremist groups have bastardized something of such beauty. However, I suppose the same could be said for the bloodshed of the Crusades or the repression of women's rights and internal pedophilia in the Catholic Church. There is no modern religion clean from the influence of greed, power, and violence. Yet another sign that there is as much to fear at home as there is abroad.

Designed by Adrian Smith of the US-based architecture firm Skidmore, Owings & Merrill, the Burj Khalifa tower stands just over a half-mile above the city. It was originally named Burj Dubai but later renamed Burj Khalifa after Sheikh Khalifa assisted the continuation of the building's development during financial hardship.

The Burj offers guests three distinct heights to view the 360-degree view of the city. We ascend to floor 124, take the stairs to the 125th floor, and step out onto the balcony. From that height, the city lights are surreal. They look like a model city created by a collector or child. The sun is just slipping out of sight on the horizon as hot tears of gratitude flood my eyes. I scan the observation deck. My best friends . . . my love . . . halfway across the world, embarking on a rare and sought-after journey. I cannot imagine my life any other way. How could I want anything more?

A Father's Fears

"What if you lose everything?"

These words hit me like a Mack truck. I'm forty-two years old and driving my folks around my new Colorado town when my father asks about my work, and I decide to be honest. It's soul crushing. The culture is toxic, the work is monotonous, and the CEO is driven purely by greed.

Then with sheer excitement and joy I proclaim, "I am working on going back to running my own firm." And then came the truck. You would have thought I told them I was thinking of bungee jumping off the Empire State Building. There was an immediate energy change in the car.

"What if you lose everything?"

Feeling bold, I challenge. "Lose what exactly?"

"Your house, your car, everything."

Feeling even more emboldened and also insulted, I say with pure indignation, "Well my car is paid off, and I can cover my mortgage working at Starbucks."

I wanted to say, "remember how I successfully ran my own firm for two years?" or "I am the most educated and arguably the most successful person in our family, don't you think I know what I am doing?" I wanted to scream, "I AM NOT YOU, AND I WILL NOT LIVE LIFE IN FEAR OF THE WHAT IFS!"

But I didn't say any of that. Instead, I politely changed the subject . . . look another mountain . . . and the drive continued uneventfully.

Why did his words sting so bad? Perhaps because they struck a chord of fear I have been trying to sever for two decades. Perhaps because they reeked of self-doubt. Perhaps because they came from the lips of the man whom I spent my life seeking approval from.

> *People decide the nature of the world at a very young age. You are praised for being a strong little kid so you invest in your strength. Or you become the smart girl. Or the funny boy. Or the pretty girl. And this works until you are about thirty years old.*
>
> *After your schooling is over, you recognize your chosen way of winning has become a trap. And a trap with diminishing rewards. You are a clown that no one will take seriously. Or you're a beauty queen who sees her looks fading. You're forced to realize your identity was a choice.*
>
> Chuck Palahniuk, *Consider This:*
> *Moments in My Writing Life after*
> *Which Everything Was Different*, pg. 64

I had a fantastic childhood. I grew up in a small, middle-class, beach town in northern Florida. It was the kind of town where everyone knew everyone. Where multigenerational families were the norm. Where kids went off to college only to return to rinse and repeat the family legacy.

I had the privilege to go on to a university of my choosing where I found a home among 200 young women that would unlock a part of my soul I never knew existed. Under the triangles of a Delta Delta Delta sign, I found the deeply embedded voice of confidence that whispered assurances that just maybe, I could take on this big world after all. And I was not the only one. The faded photos of girls who wore matching handmade t-shirts and themed costumes, went on to be global CEOs, political leaders, corporate lawyers, teachers, models, and moms. Most important, this chapter of life built the foundation of service to others that I will take to my grave.

These were the kind of friendships that time and space are erased with seconds of seeing each other. Years pass between outings with Jamie and Janice but laughter and vulnerability inevitably flow before the first drink is poured. And then there was my little sorority sister.

Erin and I could not have been more different. As my sorority house roommate, her perfect pink bed and neatly organized Martha Stewart magazines were in stark contrast to my yellow and blue haphazard side of the room. But my love and adoration for her was instant and has never faded. I was present the day she met her husband, the day they said I Do and in the hospital waiting room when her second baby came into the world. She is the kind of woman that only grows more beautiful each passing year yet has the authentic humor and charm to make me laugh out loud through a computer screen.

She is the kind of mom that books are written about, and the kind, I know, I could have only dreamed of being. Walking through a pottery barn in Winter Park with two toddlers and an infant, I watch in pure awe as she navigates a three-kid meltdown by handing the oldest a free catalogue to look through, silently places the middle child's hand in mine and places a pacifier in the infant's mouth all without interrupting her discussion with me on the great book she is reading. We are thousands of miles away these days, but I will always be grateful to be her Big.

To look at me you would believe I am a walking carbon copy of my mother, a true mini-me. But to know me is to know I have my father's stubborn nature and love of solitude. My father a career police officer, my mother a career teacher, we were the Webster definition of middle-class Americana.

My brother joined the Marines when I was three years old, and my earliest memory of him was a family visit when I was thirteen. Posing for pictures in his Marine dress uniform by pink azaleas in our backyard, I was immediately in awe of him. How brave to leave behind family and this little town for an unknown life around the world. I wondered what he had seen in his travels, who he had met, what he had experienced. I would long for the traditional, protective older brother bond that I saw in other families. I would daydream about long conversations over ice cream (or eventually beers) where he would describe worlds I had yet to see, and we would build family inside joke repertoires. But, alas, he would remain a quiet, introverted soul throughout the years, revealing only rare glimpses into the stories his memory holds. Fortunately, he would regularly show me he cared in his own unique fashion, like inviting me to join his high school JROTC class for a week at Perris Island to engage in a mock boot camp experience or the homemade Marine bulldog trophy he made for me.

Despite all I could accomplish on my own, he was able to do what I could not. He married a beautiful, fascinating woman from the Philippines who spoke multiple languages, cooks amazing meals and has now been a treasured part of our family for nearly thirty years. And they gave my parents their one and only grandchild.

Good fathers are always perceived as the backbone of the family, and mine was no exception. Stern, strong, quiet, and endlessly organized, he was the planner of great summer adventures that are still the most important parts of my childhood. With military precision he mapped out each stop and its approximate arrival and departure time. Is it any surprise that all these years later I make endless lists and plans for every important event in life—and some not so important ones?

If my father taught me to have a plan, my mother taught me to toss it out. Never-ending energy, generosity of spirit, and laughter that echoes long after it ends—these are the legacies of my mother. It was her influence that had our family pulled over on the side of a mountain in Colorado so I could touch—not just see—my first patch of snow. And of course, the first snowball came from her hand. My mother can talk to anyone, disarm and make friends in an instant. She is the woman who walks right up to celebrities and asks for a photo.

From my father, I was taught integrity, discipline, and hard work. From my mother, kindness, openheartedness, fearlessness, and football. It was my mother who took me as a mere infant to my first live game and over the years was patient enough to teach me the rules, the cheers, and the words to the alma mater.

Artistically talented as a dancer and singer, I was ironically, unequivocally shy when out of a stage spotlight. I often preferred getting lost in a book in the solitude of my room to finding friends to play with at the park. Even the dawn to dusk bike rides through the neighborhood, so common for 80s and 90s kids, were often done solo or with just one friend along for the ride. Looking back through childhood photos, you will find the number of friends at my birthday parties dwindled sharply when invites were not based on parents inviting other parents with kids in tow. As I got older, my circle got smaller but pleasantly more deeply intertwined. The friends I held close, held me equally close, and I was able to thrive in the inevitable awkwardness of adolescence. Certainly not the homecoming queen but not an outcast from the most talked about social scenes and parties either. Although I never had a long-standing high school sweetheart, I was blessed to have dates to all the dances and an abundant list of male friends to talk sports with.

Love was abundant in our home and community. It overflowed daily with both words and acts of kindness from my mother and grandmother. My homelife held the kind of stability and care that so many can only dream of. We were far from monetarily rich, but what we lacked in finances was made up in love. From years of dance and voice lessons to expensive overnight camps and competitions, from the most valued Christmas toy of the season to a car for my sixteenth birthday, what they had, they gave to me even if it took a sacrifice to do so. And yet, there was always a deep longing in my heart. A gap to be filled. Only in hindsight would I come to recognize it. I was always looking to be really seen and understood by my father.

To say a woman's relationship to herself and to other men is highly correlated to their relationship to their father is cliché. And yet, clichés are based in truth. There was never a moment when I did not know my father loved me. Nor was there ever a moment I felt abandoned by him.

He told me he loved me at all the appropriate times. He showed up at most of my childhood events. He cried at my first wedding upon seeing me dressed all in white. He stood by me when I filed for divorce. He gave me a loan with ridiculously low interest for the down payment on my first solo home. These are neither small nor taken for granted by me.

And yet, our inability to connect on a deeper level always left me feeling lonely, in need of his attention. He is a man of few words, and those words rarely hold the emotional depth my deeply sensitive soul longed for.

As a child, I wanted him to ask me about what I was studying in school or about the books I was reading. On the rare chance he asked what I wanted to be when I grew up, I wanted him to follow up with an experience so we could foster that interest together. I wanted him to take me on a ride-along in his police car or talk to me about what life in law enforcement was like. He had a twenty-year side business of a sprinkler installation company. I would have cherished learning how to build out a sprinkler system, and when he decided to retire from that, he never asked if I wanted to carry on the family business. But I would have. Later in life, I cringed when someone asked us in public what I did for a living because he never got it right. I don't know that he ever read any of my writings or even knew they existed.

At my doctoral graduation, my ex pulled one of his usual childish stunts. Upon realizing I was having my degree put in my maiden name, he flew into a rage and refused to attend the ceremony or festivities with my family. It left the day wrought with tension, ultimately ruining one of the most important days of my career and life. After the ceremony and a few quick pictures, my father, in his most conflict-averse state of mind, announced they were leaving, driving the two hours back home. They

45

did not want to stay in a house with my angry and volatile ex, and it was too late to get a hotel. As I watched their car disappear in the distance, I sank to the ground in a puddle of tears. I was devastated. I made my way to my favorite Italian restaurant, Bella Bella, and attempted to swallow both dinner and the reality that was my life. I had never felt so alone. Ordering a glass of champagne, I vowed to never feel this way again, even if that meant a vow to live life alone.

For my dad, love was simply providing for our family—which he did in every way he knew how. I will always be grateful for that. But little girls want to be seen by their fathers, to be understood, to be shown love through actions not just stability. At least that was true for me. Not even the overwhelming love and affection of my mother could replace the need I had to feel more emotional connection to and attention from my father. I needed to feel he was standing with me no matter what.

Over time, that loneliness grows into an adult's need to find male attention in a variety of healthy and unhealthy ways. From two unsuitable husbands to a years-long chase of a delusion of true love, I created habits of seeking out approval and attention in so many ways that did not serve me long-term. That's the subject of a different chapter altogether.

Ironically, I only came to realize this pattern by watching it emerge in the next generation. I have one biological niece and one second cousin who is more like a niece than a cousin. Both are fantastic young women: smart, funny, ambitious, caring, and kind. Being their Auntie Mel is one of the greatest joys of my life. I have gotten to take them on girls' trips, visit colleges, teach them yoga, talk about boys, and laugh at our own family quirks. I am proud to see a little stamp of my influence on them both, even if faint.

There are many similarities in their lives. Both are only children. Both have a set of parents that love them deeply and provide for them in every way possible. Both have loving grandparents and other family, like Auntie Mel, to dote on them additional love and affection. Both have had opportunities to attend good schools and participate in extracurricular activities of their choice. And they have excelled in all of it.

But as similar as they are in some ways, they are also vastly different. The level of emotional connection and attention between each of these girls and their fathers could not be more opposing. One is a concert companion, a fishing buddy, and a constant cheerleader. A man she not only respects and loves as a father but also as a best friend. Her young self-confidence bolstered by the steady force of acceptance and attention that was never dependent on boys her own age. They could exist or not exist in her world. At least through the most formative high school years, what mattered was the man at home who loved her.

The other, like my father, remained at arm's length and emotionally constricted. There is no question the love and pride he holds for her, and yet without that deeper connection, I see in her the same longing that I felt for so many years. And I see the impending patterns of chasing male attention to replace it. I saw it when we brushed off her early boy crazy nature as puppy love. I saw it later when social media and more serious relationships entered the picture. Watching her is like a mirror into my own soul. All I want in the world is to keep her safe from the disappointments I experienced in my own roller coaster journey, but we all have to learn life lessons in our own way, in our own time.

There is no perfect handbook for how to parent, and I am not implying in the slightest that I could write it if there was. But I do know what being lonely even when loved feels like. I do know how much women, maybe only some of us, maybe only the sensitive, need to feel seen and heard and understood by our fathers to gain the confidence to stop seeking their approval.

Which is why, at forty-two, my heart still dropped to hear my father question what I saw as the most exciting opportunity of my life. My father's words echoed in my head for months after they were spoken, always followed by a staunch argument that only I could hear. "What if you lose everything?" I had so many questions about this. What exactly is "everything"?

Physical possessions? Over my life I have owned four homes; two small, one medium, and one largeish—all relative, of course, to my middle-class size standards. I am at heart a true minimalist. A fact Randy likes to illustrate by saying I happily owned two pieces of furniture and one plate when I met him. Exaggeratory but not by much. There are hundreds, maybe thousands, of items in my current home I could live without and definitely no wish list of future physical possessions I would be heartbroken to not purchase.

What else could he mean? Randy? Fortunately, meeting this man at forty means he is fully aware and supportive of my crazy big dreams. Team Cicks (Collins & Hicks for those of you keeping score) was a nickname formed on our third date and has never wavered. We are the definition of a team, and that means we back each other up, play injured, and offer cover when needed. In other words, he's not going anywhere.

Perhaps he means my career. This makes the most sense. To my father a career is a linear path. You start at the bottom, work your way to the top (or as high as possible), and take the gold watch into retirement. In his risk averse world, a career is a thing to hold tight to, a thing that can be lost or taken from you.

For me, a career is a Bob Ross painting. The years and experiences only add layers of depth and dimension. Every mistake is actually a happy accident, lending itself to be recreated into something different but equally valuable to the landscape. There is nothing to be "lost" as experiences cannot be taken away. They are ours to own, infinitely.

What I came to realize years later was his fear was based in a fear of financial instability. A fear so prevalent it overshadowed every decision made for our family.

Multicolored Ghosts

They stood over six feet tall against the back wall of our garage. I can't recall the day they arrived, but I will never forget the day they were hauled away. Three full-size arcade games—*Mario Brothers*, *Scorpion*, and the prized possession, *Ms. Pac-Man*—representing so much more than their red joysticks and brown, faux-wood exterior. From atop a wooden stool with a tan leather cushion, I spent hours playing, competing, laughing with my father. While my mom could hold her own at the game, it was the rare daddy/daughter time I treasured. As the yellow circle with a pink bow ate dots and ran from multicolor ghosts, I giggled and my dad smiled. Whether mere moments or full hours, it felt like time stopped. It was an unforgettable slice of childhood that even thirty years later compels me to stop and play anytime I see a machine.

And then one day, a man in a truck with a dolly arrived and slowly wheeled them away. Upon my inquiry, I was reminded that our RV had broken down on our recent summer vacation in Canada and the repairs were expensive. Selling these was the best way to pay off the credit card debt. I went to my room in the far corner of the house and cried. I am certain this action was brushed off as that of a spoiled child. After all, I couldn't possibly understand the adult decisions that must be made for our family. And didn't I have the latest Nintendo in my room that I could play? But I already knew what I couldn't articulate. It wasn't about the game; it was the closing of a chapter of connection with my father that would never be replaced.

Like many things in our society, money is a subject deemed unsuitable to discuss in most situations, especially for women. But it is, by far, one of the most complex and emotionally charged relationships we will ever have as humans. More than any word or even deed, the choices on where and how to earn and spend money are a direct representation of our values. Whether those values are instant gratification or a means to a longer-term end, financial choices are life's continuous trade off.

The most precursory glance into my finances illuminates three overwhelming values: travel, education, and service. For more than two decades, the majority of my disposable income has been spent experiencing the world, from the mundane and domestic to the foreign and exotic. Travel has proven to be a priceless commodity to who I am as a human, teaching me culture and traditions, vulnerability and openheartedness, creativity and solitude. I have been privileged to witness the best of humanity and the evil remnants of the worst. While I am still a believer in responsible retirement planning and investing, I also believe each and every experience I have used my precious capital to provide is an investment in my future self, albeit of a different kind— the intrinsic kind that can neither be fully explained nor fully appreciated by anyone but me. It is my literal take on *you only live once.*

Along with education found through experience, I also value education directly. After the good fortune of a fully paid undergraduate degree, I used my own finances to support a master's and doctoral degree. This decision left me strapped with student loan debt far into my adult life, leaving some to question the return on investment. However, I have never regretted one second of that decision. My master's degree provided practical business lessons I have used in consultancy for the last thirteen years, while my doctorate degree taught me research and technical writing, where I learned I was a natural grant writer. When people ask me if a college degree is still worth the price, I always give the same answer: a college degree costs roughly the same amount as a car, whether you choose economy or luxury. However, a car you have for five to seven years; your education you have for a lifetime. What may seem to some as a few insignificant letters by my name has given credibility, opened doors, ignited connections, and laid the literal foundation for everything I have become.

The third pillar of my financial choices is deeply rooted in my version of serving others. Every year, I work to give 20-25% of my resources to causes I care about. I have neither the means nor the inclination to give that as one big check deserving the honor on a donor board. Rather, I look for organic small ways to give that add up to be more than a sum of their parts. And I give with ferocious intentionality. I support social enterprise businesses as often as possible, opting to pay extra even if the item could be found cheaper on Amazon. I watch for initiatives of friends working in the nonprofit sector to support directly. I allow myself to splurge on charity silent auction items I normally would never afford. Sometimes this looks like picking up a tab for a friend in need, even when money was tight. Or fighting to pay a check I really couldn't afford because my wealthier friend had picked up the last three. There are lean years when the amount I have to give is small but there is never a question that sacrifices will be made in other places in order to keep this value a priority. There are robust years when I can proudly give more. The amount is irrelevant, giving is all that matters.

I am certainly not alone in my skirmish with limiting emotions around finances. It is estimated that there are 114% more female entrepreneurs in the US today than twenty years ago; however, 90.3% of them are micro-businesses (aka side hustles) that never grow to full financial prosperity. (Fundera.com) A search on Amazon for books on women and money will return more than 80,000 results. So, what is it that gives women, including myself, such a dysfunctional relationship with the almighty dollar?

> *I would rather show my breasts in public than my bank statement! It appears somehow that my sexual liberation has bounded ahead of my liberation around money.*
>
> Louise Tarrier,
> *Women's Relationship with Money,*
> TreeSisters Blog

It's Complicated

In her January 2020 article *The Complicated Relationship Between Women and Money,* Jamie Burton highlights some well-known facts: women earn less money, take more time out of the workforce, and tend to outlive their male counterparts. But any woman who has ever really been serious about their independent financial future also knows there is more to it than that.

In fact, a Social Indicators Research 2015 study by Furnham et. al found that women are far more likely to associate money with love and therefore give larger percentages of their resources as a show of generosity. In contrast, men were more likely to associate money with power and exhibit hoarding tendencies with personal wealth.

Money for me is an ever-evolving relationship and one I will likely always struggle with. There are days I feel unworthy when I witness the wealth others have built, knowing I had opportunities to do the same but somehow failed. There are days I feel guilty about money decisions that don't fall in to my three aforementioned value categories. There are days I feel conflicted when I pay off all my debt only to immediately give into the urge to book another international adventure or give another donation I shouldn't really afford.

In the end, like everything else we absorb from our upbringing, there comes a time in life when we have to take a fresh look at the childhood lessons we carry into adulthood. Were they true wisdom or old wives' tales? Are they still relevant in modern times we live? Do they still serve us in the way our life uniquely unfolded? Did they ever really feel right in the first place? Only we can decide what tools to keep in our toolkit and which to discard. The most important thing is the process of intentional examination and guilt-free release of what no longer serves us.

The Yellow Dot Return

In the end, I did make the leap to start my own company, and eventually a second. I have never regretted it. As lonely as it was to go alone, sometimes that is the path we must take to follow our own dreams. I'll perhaps never know how much quiet judgment or anxiety this caused my father as he will likely never share. Like so many of our family's deepest emotions, they might escape in a comment here or there but are mostly kept tightly locked in the boxes of our collective family attic.

> *Should is how other people want us to live our lives. It's all of the expectations that others layer upon us. Sometimes, Shoulds are small, seemingly innocuous, and easily accommodated. "You should listen to that song," for example. At other times, Shoulds are highly influential systems of thought that pressure and, at their most destructive, coerce us to live our lives differently.*

> Elle Luna,
> *The Crossroads of Should and Must:*
> *Find and Follow Your Passion*, pg.29

Somewhere along life's path I came to accept that having my father's approval doesn't mean walking the same road he did. In fact, being the best combination of my parents while forging my own path is perhaps the best honor I could ever give them. Being my full self means chasing the biggest, scariest dreams I can conjure. It means loving the people I love, whether or not they approve. It means making my own mistakes and being OK with the consequences. It means leaving behind their ideas about what a life or a career is supposed to look like and standing strong for the reality of mine.

> *Success is to know who you are, to walk through life being considerate of others, and spend our time giving back. Success comes from within. To me, it's about being rich in love and life.*

> Dominique Crenn,
> Interview with *Vanity Fair* Magazine,
> September 2021

And then, just when you think you have your family figured out, they surprise you. More than thirty years after those multi-colored ghosts were hauled away from our garage, a texted picture from my mom would send me straight to tears. There, on the backwall of their garage, sat a brand-new Pac-Man machine. On an uncharacteristic whim, my dad bought it just in time for my summer visit. As I stepped out of the car, I was instantly transported to my ten-year-old self. There sat a wooden stool and a yellow circle to eat dots. I was, once again, on a mission to connect with my dad and set the high score while I was at it.

I am startled back to reality with a pull toward a group photo and a lively discussion about dinner plans. As we descend the 125 stories I think of a particular irony. My parents instilled in me this wanderlust to explore yet they themselves have barely left North America. Many years previous, I stopped telling them where I was going until after the fact, or perhaps the day prior. A coping mechanism to methodically avoid the projection of their own fears that was sure to fall on me each time I chose to travel somewhere exotic. However, these days I am proud to talk about my adventures. Proud of the combination of stubborn independence, endless wanderlust, and naive fearlessness that drives me to drink in the world, one country at a time. Proud to be learning how to live out my daydreams every single day.

Chapter 3:
Kathmandu

Altitude: 1,300m/4,264ft
Travel Time: Four hour flight
Soundtrack: 23, Sam Hunt

The flight from Dubai to Kathmandu is a short four hours. Still buzzing from our Dubai excursion, we are met immediately with a stark reality: the airport is small, crowded, and not air-conditioned. The process to proceed out to the city is a tedious, multi-hour one. Grateful for our Nepalese friend and group leader for translation, we navigate obtaining Nepalese cash to purchase a visa, wait for approval, and then proceed to baggage to claim our bags. The group sits restlessly or paces around. The first reality check on the lack of internet and phone service this trip will entail.

Once processed, we fight the airport crowd to board a small van and head into the heart of the city. As we depart, we see a group of wild monkeys have gathered on the rocks just to the left of our van, as if to send us off. The surreal nature of the scene gives us all a chuckle as the theme song from *The Jungle Book* plays in my head.

We arrive in downtown Kathmandu with its narrow, bustling streets and spiderweb of electrical cords. Our hotel looks like a castle rising out of the city's chaotic heart.

Kathmandu, Nepal's capital, is set in a valley surrounded by the Himalayan mountains. At the heart of the old city's maze-like alleys is Durbar Square, which becomes frenetic during Indra Jatra, a religious festival featuring masked dances.

The city has become the country's most important business and commercial center through the efforts of Newar merchant families. In the 1970s, the construction of new roads and the expansion of air service were centered upon Kathmandu, making it the hub of the national transportation system, which for centuries was limited to footpaths.

On April 25, 2015, a magnitude-7.8 earthquake struck central Nepal, its epicenter about fifty miles northwest of Kathmandu. Initial estimates on how many people had been killed in the country by the quake were more than 1,500, but that number quickly grew as rescue and recovery workers reached more-remote locations. In all, some 9,000 people died and about 16,800 were injured by the main quake and numerous aftershocks. Kathmandu was severely damaged, especially the buildings in its historic center, and tens of thousands were made homeless. Durbar Square's palace, Hanuman Dhoka, and Kasthamandap, a wooden Hindu temple, are still being rebuilt.

The Newar, who comprise about half the population of the Kathmandu Valley in Nepal, speak a language belonging to the Tibeto-Burman family, but their culture has been strongly influenced by Indian religious and social institutions. The Newar population of Nepal was estimated to be about 1,250,000 in the early twenty-first century. Most of the Newar are Hindus, but some practice an Indian form of Buddhism.

The Newar have a wide range of occupations. Many are farmers; others are prominent in the retail trades; and some occupy high political and administrative posts. They have traditionally been noted as architects and artisans, the builders of the famous temples and shrines of Kathmandu. From the tenth to sixteenth century, painting and sculpture flourished among the Newar, along with crafts such as pottery making, paper production, wood carving, and metallurgy. Each of the crafts has traditionally been the specialty of a particular caste.

Kathmandu's early name was Manju-Patan. The origins of the present-day Kathmandu refers to a wooden temple (*kath*, "wood;" *mandir*, "temple" or "edifice") said to have been built from the wood of a single tree by Raja Lachmina Singh in 1596.

We embark on a full day city tour around Kathmandu Valley including Kathmandu city, the city of monuments, temples, and monasteries such as Durbar Square, Bouddhanath, and Swoyambhunath. As we pass a park full of kids playing cricket, my mind wanders to my own obsession with America's pastime.

America's Past Time

The crinkle of the hot dog foil is overshadowed by the crack of the ball against the bat. It's the top of the ninth and the Cubs are getting smoked 11-4 by the Orioles. But I'm in no rush to leave. The beer I bought just before cut-off is still cold, and the summer heat is countered by a rare breeze. It's 2008, seven years before the curse was broken, and I'm in Wrigley Field heaven.

I love baseball stadiums. I've seen a Major League game in twenty of them on my hunt for all thirty-two. Traveling the country, many times alone, just to be in the atmosphere—it's the architecture and the food and the people watching. From stoic red brick at Camden Yards to the salty air of San Francisco Bay wafting outside Oracle Park. It's hot dogs and giant beers at the White Sox to the chocolate covered strawberries and bison burgers at the Rockies. It's postgame shenanigans in Wrigleyville and pregame tailgating with stranger-turned-friend Brewers fans. All of it excites me.

The old Atlanta Braves stadium was my first. An eight-hour bus ride with thirty-five other teens, I remember very little about this except it was a church trip, and I sat next to a boy who could play guitar. But it sparked a love of stadiums that would follow me throughout my life. I planned weekends alone, joined acquaintances I barely knew, took my nieces to their first game, and made it to one ESPN Sports Center highlight reel.

But here's the thing: I don't enjoy the game of baseball. Don't ask me stats, batting averages, star players, or even divisions—I won't know. But I could tell you how comfortable the seats were, the part of the stadium with the best food, whether the mascot is a good entertainer or not. I can tell you if the crowd energy is high or subdued and how much of it is fueled by beers. All the things I love about baseball have nothing to do with the game.

Like so many things in my life, it is the thrill of the chase that keeps me coming back time and time again. It is a kind of alive that I can never quite feel in any other way. There is simply something intoxicating about putting my whole self into the uncomfortable, being fully immersed in the scenes and energy. It is something I cannot get by reading or studying or hearing from others. I have to be there, live and in person, to feel it for myself.

Over the years I have chased many things: twenty baseball stadiums, close to a hundred concerts, dozens of international countries—but only once was that chase human. The Great Chase. The unattainable white rabbit who flitted in and out of my life for years daring me to continue down the rabbit hole. Once was enough to know the return on investment would never equate to the price to be paid. And yet I kept paying long after I should have stopped.

The White Rabbit

I was twenty-three years old when it began. Sporting my favorite pair of jeans and a school spirit green and orange T-shirt, I casually strolled the main hall of Jenkins Building. A 1960s design, Jenkins stands out on campus as the eyesore from the classic brick beauties that surround her. She smells equal parts aged oak and recently mopped linoleum.

I was relatively new in town but diving right into my familiar place as a volunteer leader. On this day, as the newly elected student ambassador, I was deeply preoccupied with the speech I was to give in the coming hours. I looked up just in time to lock eyes.

The Herbert Business School is many things but a haven for the handsome is not one of them, making this moment seem to proceed in slow motion. He was slim and tan, with a stride unassuming yet confident. I felt myself stand a little taller as I walked past, something intrinsically electric in the air. Involuntarily, I turned around, and to my surprise, so had he. I turned back and walked on, letting out a giggle reminiscent of a preteen.

An hour later, the moment long passed, I stepped into the room to give my welcome speech to see him sitting front and center in the audience. We locked eyes again, and my cheeks flushed red as he flashed me a broad, all-knowing smile.

In the years that followed, he would become many things in my life; yet nothing more impactful than a reality check on what the ebb and flow of affection can look like, feel like. And the scars it can leave behind.

From South Carolina gazebos to Montgomery hotel bars; basement card games to swanky city restaurants, we were never a couple, always just friends. But friends who became much more. Friends who seesawed between baring our souls and barely knowing each other.

It was a friendship that put as many miles on my car as it did my heart, with a soundtrack long enough to travel cross-country without repeat. A friendship filled with as many secrets and inside jokes as tears and heartbreak. A friendship that left me equally satisfied and longing. A friendship that brought me out of darkness and called me on my immaturity, sometimes in the same sentence. A friendship made up of a million tiny moments haphazardly strung together over years.

We can convince ourselves of many things when we really want to believe them. That we are different. That we are special. That we are more. That we are important. That it is equitable. That it is meant to be. That the timing is just off. That one day, it will be enough. That it is love. And then one day you wake up and realize you may have made him a main character in your mind's story, but you were always just supporting cast.

There is a fine line between visioning and delusion. The former a powerful tool for success; the latter a powerful tool for failure. During those years, I carefully walked the tightrope between the two. Believing in an inevitability of a faraway outcome that had no evidence of reality. Ignoring my obvious low priority status. Allowing the thrill of the chase to dull the pain of disappointment. Carefully tiptoeing around the recognition that it was a delusion all along. And it was certainly a delusion. Despite his words, I was neither a priority nor singular in his life. But for a little while, I reveled in the sheer deliciousness of that delusion.

Author Jen Pastiloff uses the phrase "fall-in-lovable" in her workshops to illustrate the way we can deeply connect with others if they allow us to see them at their most vulnerable. And seeing them in this state does not require them to feel the same reciprocally. This is exactly how I fell in love with him. His normal demeanor was aloof and hard to read. He seemed to own the world around him with intimidating grace. But every so often he shared with me a rare, vulnerable glimpse into the inner workings of his heart and mind. At a depth just enough, and a frequency just enough, to make me fall in love with him again, and keep me longing to know more.

Love is a many-splendored thing. I have loved many people in my lifetime. I love my husband and stepdaughter. I love my family, both immediate and distant. I have loved two ex-husbands and a handful of boyfriends. I have loved two former stepchildren. I have loved friends and children of friends. I have loved strangers and those in need. Love is the act of offering a piece of yourself to someone else. Through words or deeds, it's an external output that you hope makes that person's life better.

But being in love is different. Unlike the selflessness that defines love, being in love is selfish, autonomous, and intimate. Being in love is fully internal and personal. It's about a soul swirling so dramatic it makes you dizzy. It's butterflies and connective energy; swooning in the aura of someone or something. It has all the unicorn and rainbow features of infatuation but it's deeper, more grounded, and somehow more knowing. This is a feeling I have known only twice in my life. He was the first.

From him I gained a love/hate relationship with the sunrise. When I was alone, sunrise stood for the elation in beginning again, the tranquility of a quieted world, the ecstasy of nature's beauty. When I was with him, sunrise brought on the gray haze of another goodbye. Another ending without closure. Another ambiguous period of intense longing. Another trip to rebab to fight the withdrawal symptoms from one of my life's only drugs. Forcefully reminding myself that anything that happens in the night—any words spoken, emotions whispered, intimacy shared—will disappear like an oasis in the desert. Somewhere between it never happened or he wished it hadn't.

There were hundreds of party nights, where booze and unrequited desire flowed. There were private nights where no desire was unrequited. So many nights I believed in the words, the actions, the intentions. So many mornings I awoke to the retreat, the regret, the rejection.

The truth is, he made no promises. In fact, despite adventures galore, we never even went on a single real date. We rarely acknowledged the pull and push of our friendship, choosing to cover with silence instead. But I knew the roller coaster it was doing to my emotions, even if I wanted to pretend not to.

Some days our friendship was simple and comfortable . . .

He was waiting on the wooden picnic table in his backyard when I arrived with a late lunch in hand. We chatted the afternoon away with football and politics before the conversation gained depth. Both processing through our respective divorces, we said more with our eyes than we articulated in words. There was a tension between us that was as emotional as it was sexual. We both knew we were checking in. How were we really holding up? It was in these moments that I believed no one else in the world could understand me, really see me, the way he did. And somewhere deep down, I believed the reverse was also true.

But these were fleeting moments. In an instant, a glance at his watch would propel us back to reality. He had to get ready for the evening; the babysitter would arrive soon. I knew better than to inquire what he had to get ready for. It made no difference what her name was. It ached the same.

Other days our friendship was a string of drunken, comical, amusements . . .

He was out of town on a birthday extravaganza. I was home laughing through a barrage of texts daring me to join.

"Get here." "Come on, don't be scared." "Book it—I'll pay for it. Here's my credit card."

Knowing this merry-go-round far too well, I waited for morning light to divest myself from the game.

Me: Exactly how many women did you send your credit card to last night?! 😊😊

Him: Cracking up!

Me: So, I get in at 9:28 on DL 3771. Are you picking me up or sending directions?

Him: Funny

Me: What's funny?

Him: You cannot come here!! That would be bad, bad, bad!!

Me: Well, you should have thought of that before sending me your credit card shouldn't you?

Him: I didn't think you'd take that seriously.

Me: I am fucking with you doll—of course I didn't!!!!

And then there were days I was reminded of my own delusion . . .

It was a familiar scene of friends gathered in a downstairs den to share beer and laughter, music and mischief. The crowd included the usual crew: the guys, me, and new girls-du-jour. A strip poker game ensued with forced physical vulnerability as laughable as it was sensual. As the night grew late, the girls went home, and the guys retired to guest rooms. I was dozing on the couch, wondering how long to sober up before I made the one-mile drive home. Equally wondering if, once the house was quiet, he would share in my desire to get loud.

Then I heard it, the ping of a message on his phone, the tapping of his fingers on a reply, murmur of his voice to one of the guys, and the turn of the car engine. He was gone. And I was alone, dozing on his couch, feeling deeply foolish. Knowing it was unsafe to drive, I debated the walk home. Neither barefoot nor in the heels I was carrying seemed a viable option for walking that distance on these historic neighborhood cobblestones. It was hard to discern if the look on his face was more shocked or annoyed to find me still there when he returned at dawn. We never spoke of it.

Soul Training

Sometimes I look back and scold myself for my own foolishness, but then I give my soul grace, knowing it would serve me later somehow.

It's funny, really, when a rational mind gets involved. There was so much we didn't know of one another, and yet somehow when we were together it felt like we knew everything. I couldn't tell you what car he drove as a teen, his favorite color, or the brand of toothpaste he bought. But I knew there was once a pile of yellow legal pads full of deep thoughts in the corner of his basement. I knew he was deeply affected by the life he once lived before becoming the executive he is now. I know his oldest went through a dinosaur phase, and I read him the same book no less than ten times one Saturday. I know the nervous excitement he had while sipping coffee with me before the interview that would change his career. I know he once loved sunny-side-up eggs. I know he once shared my dream of writing a book. I know he chose the picket fence but sometimes dreams of the wilder days. I know he fears aging because he's tied it to irrelevance. I know what whiskey tasted like on his lips and how his hand felt on the small of my back.

Accepting that dual divorces would not result in the golden ticket to ride off together into the sunset took an Ironman of soul training. But then I met a sweet man who accepted my still-healing scars and made me genuinely laugh. Over our three years together, we would move north and he would begin to chip away at this long held fantasy I was still holding onto. Slowly but steadily, I began to quietly lay my demons to rest in the glow of acceptance and mature adoration. Until I made a critical mistake of looking in the rearview mirror.

I had moved out of town just six months when the all too familiar digital ding sent my heart aflutter all over again.

Him: This place sucks without you.

And just like that, pandora's box reopened.

My memory fails me when I attempt to recall what made me believe this next scenario would be less than disastrous. The man I spent the previous three years trying to get out of my psyche, inviting me and my new boyfriend to join him, his new girlfriend, and all the old party gang to the place where we once shared the delicious elixir of alcohol, chaos, emotions, and sex. Did I not see the inevitability that old flames would reignite old longings?

Him: You know...

Me: What? Tell me

Him: Nothing...

Me: Come on—don't hold back. We don't hold secrets

Him: Dump him and marry me

Me: In a heartbeat

Him: It's always been you. This can all be yours. You can make all these girls disappear. Just sayin…

Me: If you were serious, you know I would

Him: Mel, I love you

Me: Ditto, I have been in love with you since the day we met

Him: It should be us. How'd we mess it all up

In Hollywood, these words would have held the depth of vulnerability that leads two people into a tangle of sensual desire for the night before escaping together in a ride into the sunset. But life, unfortunately, is not a movie, and just as easily as these vulnerable words fell onto digital paper, they were erased by the morning light.

> *Someone once said to me, "Life is not a fairy tale. If you lose a shoe at midnight, you are drunk, not a princess."*

M. Jewsbury,
Because I Love Him, pg. 55

Taking the Shot

Funny thing about energy: when you build your career on drawing people to you, you get a lot of interesting results. Years after I was certain this chapter of life was closed for good, a text reconnecting us would begin the slow opening of our pandora's box of friendship. A box I was certain I had welded shut. A journey down this rabbit hole would once again lead to rekindling conversations filled with foggy memories and wistful future plans. And then the invitation. He was coming back to South Florida and wanted to get together, catch up over coffee. Even after many years of drifted silence, this simple invitation had the power to create an involuntary anticipatory enthusiasm. Who was he now? How was his new career? How were the kids? Is he writing or thinking of writing? There were so many things I wanted to ask, and even more I wanted to share. My own new career and life. How far I have come, and the road I have planned.

But I knew better than to dance with old ghosts. I knew better than to believe in ghosts at all. As with all the night conversations prior, morning light would lead again to ghostly quiet and faded intentions. He just couldn't make the time on this trip. Maybe next time. Luckily, disappointment that once took days or weeks to pass over, now took mere hours.

So, what is it that makes one profess their love at night and deny it in the morning? Once or twice might be chalked up to alcohol. But to engage in this ritual for years?

Perhaps these words were all meaningless gestures. Things one says for a reaction to expand an ego. Was I simply the girl so wrapped up in the ecstasy of his aura that he knew he could recharge his ego with my ever-present adoration? Or were they truths let out of the vault in a slow night leak, only to be sealed back in each morning?

Over the years I have pondered many potentials. Perhaps I was too simple, failing to offer the dynamic power player to match the corporate and wealth world he circulated through. Perhaps it was physical and the attraction I felt was one sided, me not quite as beautiful as I hoped he'd see. Perhaps I was too wild, unsuitable for the picket fence life he desired. Too tarnished to be accepted by his family and friends. He witnessed the worst chapter of my life, the worst version of me. The broken version yet to be welded with gold into the beautiful kintsugi bowl I eventually healed into. Perhaps one can never come back from that. I am astonished anyone could have loved that girl.

It is a fruitless endeavor to continually ponder the whys of life after so many years. We need only to be reminded of the realities. If he'd ever come for me, I would have followed. But he never did.

And, if I am honest, thank God he didn't.

To be sure there would be fabulously frivolous adventures and ecstasy filled trysts to remember but would it equal all I found elsewhere? It is doubtful. The truth would look much more like domesticity and a completely different chase. An endless chase for his attention, for his connection, for his inner vault. I would have allowed my life to be wrapped into his passions, his work, his plans. I would have followed a path of least resistance into whatever life he wanted us to have. Would that have settled down my wanderlust or left me wanting more?

In the end, my life would hold a fraction of its magic had we run off into the sunset together as I once dreamed. So many people I would have never met; places I would have never seen; so many ways I would not have given back to the world. So many tears of joy and nights of laughter I would never know. So much of the gritty, rich depth of my perfectly imperfect life would never have manifested.

Nearly twenty years to the day the great chase began, I bellied up to a bar with an old friend who witnessed it all. Prompted by his own great chase, we pondered the "what if" versus "oh well" debate. The philosophical life debate between following your heart or spend your life wondering what could have been.

Do we only fall in love with the idea of a person rather than the real person? If you miss your window of opportunity, can you ever go back? How much are you willing to give up for the chance to have it all? Are some connections only desirous because of the mystery, the chase? Why do some always run? Why do others continue to chase?

The questions were endless, our beers were not.

As we hit the bottom of our glasses, I offered my two cents. When given the choice, I will always err on the side of taking the shot when life hands you the ball. After all, if you miss, you only become stronger. Or, like the great chase, once you move past the what ifs, you can relish the lessons learned.

Re-closing the box on this life chapter and climbing the ladder to place it back in my mind's attic, I had a revelation. I never gave enough gratitude to the role the great chase played in who I became, how I chose to live, and how I chose to love. When facing unrequited love, we lose our control over the outcome. We are left hungry and longing. Perhaps this life chapter laid the groundwork for my insistence on seeing life as an adventure to be enjoyed. When you seek adventure, it is never unrequited. When you become fearlessly independent, no one but you can let you down.

In her poem, "The Uses of Sorrow," Mary Oliver says, "Someone I loved once gave me a box full of darkness. It took me years to understand that this, too, was a gift."

These days I chase summit highs on Colorado 14ers, largemouth bass in Georgia Lakes, and ambitious dreams on global stages. But I think often of the great chase and just smile, grateful for all the moments we were somewhere between real love and real life.

We closed out our day in Kathmandu in a New Orleans-style restaurant. Having deep connection to both my Cajun family roots and New Orleans specifically, the irony of this particular theme is not lost on me. You can fly halfway across the world to chase an adventure and a dream. You can thrive on the thrill of the chase. Yet something will always bring you back. We never really escape the pieces of life that made us who we are. Truthfully, I wouldn't want to.

Chapter 4:
Ramechhap

Altitude: 1,218m/3,996ft
Travel Time: Four hours by van
Soundtrack: You, Lucy Daydream

With the Kathmandu airport partially under construction, we are unable to travel to Lukla directly. Our guides arrange transport to the Ramechhap Region, a four-hour van ride away, to reroute from the small, regional airport.

Ramechhap District, a part of Bagmati Province, is also known as Kirat Ramechhap, with Manthali as its district headquarters.

Considered a rural district, the people from Ramechhap and its surrounding district visit the Manthali market to shop for spices and other basic ingredients. Students looking for a greater education will travel the distance from their home at Ramechhap to Manthali. The district has the highest population of Kusunda, the native group considered endangered with the lowest population growth rate in Nepal.

Traditional hotels and accommodations are scarce in this region so visitors are primarily relegated to the various campsites available throughout. However, the district continues to be popular with visitors due to is plentiful religious and cultural sites including several monasteries.

Khandadevi, built with ancient stone walls, is a fascinating Hindu temple of goddess Khanda Devi. In 1458, a shepherd built this temple in Ramechhap, and it is now the most prominent cultural site of the district. Some believe the popularity is heightened out of curiosity for the former practice of animal sacrifice to impress the goddess into listening to the devotee's prayers.

Other popular religious sites of Ramechhap District are the ponds of Panch Pokhari and Jatapokhari. On average, each year more than 3,000 visitors set off on a pilgrimage to these ponds. Visitors dip in the holy waters to fulfill their wishes during the period of Janaipurnima annually in August and September.

The Numbur Cheese Circuit is a popular new trek in the district. The trek gets its name for Nepal's first cheese factories, established in 1957, that fall along the route. Starting at Shivalaya, some adventurers utilize this location to begin their Everest Base Camp trek, particularly if they do not wish to risk the dangerous flight to Lukla. The recommended schedule for the trek takes fourteen days of trekking, although at a push it can be completed in up to ten days by combining some of the shorter days. It can also be extended several days for those who wish to visit some of the nearby glaciers, peaks, or lakes. The excursion provides astonishing views of major Himalayan peaks including Annapurna South, Langtang, Gaurishankar, and Numburchuili, as well as walks through deep river gorges, glacial lakes, terraced rice fields, subtropical forests, and Sherpa villages to the Lhiku Khola glacier.

Despite these religious and cultural attractions, our group is headed to the region for the sole purpose of getting to Lukla to begin the trek. As we make our way on the bumpy, four-hour van ride, I watch the countryside whiz by and realize there is something oddly nostalgic to this ride. Years earlier, I had taken a similar four-hour van ride from Moscow to Kolomna; a trip equally fraught with danger and mysticism.

Smoky Reflections

Russia in 2010 is everything and nothing like I pictured it. We arrive in a gray fog of choking smoke from wildfires burning all over the country, out of control. It is a national disaster here yet the world media, including and especially the American media, have scarcely mentioned it. The Russian government is fighting among itself on how to best proceed. Too proud to ask for help from other countries and too centralized in their government structure to work entrepreneurially, the regions affected watch helplessly as thousands of acres are burned, human lives are lost, and citizens wait day after endless day in the smoky heat.

The infrastructure of roads and buildings are dilapidated and crumbling, literally resembling the antiquated relics leftover after cold war disenfranchising. If I didn't know better, I might think this country was liberated a few months ago rather than a few decades. I see more broken-down cars in three days in Russia than I have in years of American driving. Smoking is allowed everywhere, and I laugh at the irony of a nonsmoking section at the hotel restaurant that immediately abuts the smoking table next to it. This must have been what the 1970s and 80s were like in the US.

Yet in a strange irony, the Russian service industry takes great pride in cleanliness. At restaurants, the plates and glasses are cleared with such efficiency I have started to feel they have sensors alerting them to emptiness. The housekeeping staff works around the clock constantly dusting, mopping, sweeping, causing a hint of my own self-conscious nature to straighten my scattered clothes in the hotel room.

There is little air conditioning in Russia, a fact that most years would scarcely be noticed, but this summer a scorching heat wave, Russia's hottest in recorded history, leaves buildings, including my own hotel room, feeling more like a sauna than a quiet place of rest.

I have taken to sleeping in the hotel game room, a large room off the lobby with two eastern-style air conditioners. I curl up on the small rug at the back of the room and feel my body temperature slowly decline to a restful state. I stay there until around five a.m., and then make my way back to my room to finish off the morning.

On the third day of this strange ritual, I walk down the hall back toward the room and feel drawn to the open window at the end of the hall. I look out and, although there is still smoke, it looks different. The air feels cool, almost crisp. I change into workout clothes but stop short of the basement gym, venturing instead outdoors to enjoy the inviting air. It is just past six a.m.

For three hours, I wander around the property taking in every detail. There is a garden to the left of the hotel with an uncomfortable raw wood swing. I sit in it for over an hour and watch small apples fall from an abundantly ripe tree above. There are vegetables growing in a small greenhouse and flowers blooming in a variety of colors. Beyond the garden is a picnic area with a traditional gazebo. There is a fountain with a happy, comical frog, a winding path to the riverside, and boats parked quietly in the marina—all things I had neglected to notice until now. There are endless seating areas meant for cozy conversation or perhaps self-reflection.

I giggle a nervous apology as I walk around back of the hotel and nearly bump into a large Russian woman wearing the turquoise housekeeping uniform resembling hospital scrubs sweeping the outdoor patio then stopping for a smoke break.

While I wander I listen to an audio version of Elizabeth Gilbert's *Eat, Pray, Love* and feel incredibly inspired—to write, to pray, to meditate—just as Elizabeth Gilbert intended I am certain.

For years, Gilbert has been my icon and distant mentor. From the depths with which she bares her soul in her writing to the way she brings it back from the dark to a light of inspiration. But no topic better aligns with my life than that of being a childless woman. In her 2016 *TIME* magazine interview, she articulates my life story in a single paragraph.

> *There's certainly still this idea that you're meant to look on these women [without children] with pity and horror...What if somebody instead is free to joyfully pursue one really interesting path after another, and to be calm and happy enough to celebrate everyone else's choices while totally digging her own? That's the model I didn't see growing up. And I wish I could have shown myself that. I think it would have made her jaw drop.*

For much of the previous few years, I felt restless and unhappy. I blamed it on weather, but I know that was only partially true. Florida had become too hot for me—physically and metaphorically. I felt as debilitated by the heat as I did my own life there. I began to actively search out opportunities elsewhere. I felt a great connection to Colorado when I visited there. Was that the answer? How about abroad? Was that possible? What would I do for work? Where would I go? Am I searching or simply running away? I was not sure, but the growing upheaval in my soul was a sure sign something must change soon.

In that moment, however, here I was . . . in Russia. Officially here to watch the man I was dating compete in the World Canopy Piloting Championships, while in reality, for much more. I marvel at the idea as I leave my bench and wander down to the riverside beach and its course, grainy, tan sand.

Canopy Piloting, a small and relatively fledgling sport, is the maverick of skydiving. "Swooping," as it is referred to in slang, requires a skill and control level unmatched by any other discipline. It is a sport that had captured my fascination since being introduced to it a few months earlier—both for its complexity and its danger. It is the only spectator friendly skydiving discipline, and I wonder often why it has not grown more rapidly in popularity with audiences. It is so foreign a sport to me that it ignites an excitement resembling a child waiting for Santa.

As the gravy-thick smoke finally clears, the clouds make an opening and the sun to beams down as happily as the Dalai Lama's endless smile. The houses across the airfield are now in view at last, and their unique beauty looks even more appealing after this withheld revelation. They have green and orange shutters and tattered roofs. The airfield itself is an aviation graveyard with rows of aging planes and helicopters, mostly WWII military, in various levels of reconstruction. A local pilot later told us that at the fall of the USSR, those with the skills to fly and wherewithal to understand future capitalism basically staked their personal claim to any and all government owned items including old military planes to turn into private transport and other entrepreneurial endeavors.

To everyone's amazement the smoke stays at bay, and the competition ensues on schedule over the next few days. There are eighteen countries represented at this year's World Championships, and flags of each are hung at the various packing tents in a friendly yet territorial way. The competitor's spirits are high—even after mediocre runs—just to be finally taking a breath of fresh air. The teamwork and camaraderie warms the heart as fierce competitors will take time to give the proverbial high five and "rip it up." The downtime gives grand opportunities to really get to know one another. It is easy to see how this can become as addicting of a social scene as it is a sport.

As an outsider, I rarely, if ever, feel unwelcome or inadequate, even in this close-knit, family atmosphere. The density of the sport and intricacies of its equipment rivals any; yet, the team seems to enjoy taking time to explain the details to me, and I am an equally appreciative listener.

The competition ends with a celebration day complete with a freestyle swooping competition, a flocking dive, and a very close airplane flyby. All to entertain the few hundred spectators that have come to participate. Emotions of pride, accomplishment, disappointment, and self-doubt wind their way through the hearts and minds of the competitors that took part. The famed "Tiger Woods of Canopy piloting" takes yet another World Championship title back to Canada while Team USA took the prize for most medals of any country. Russia, notoriously dangerous and unskilled in this sport, claimed their very first medal, delighting the hometown crowd.

Following the closing ceremonies, a banquet of food is laid out and the party begins. I spend a long and interesting twenty minutes in the company of a fellow American who serves as chief judge for the competition. She is a fascinating woman, as knowledgeable and insightful as she is intriguing. I ask her about her life outside of skydiving, and she tells me about her passion for endangered animals and her work with African free roaming dogs. I express my gratitude for being able to be a guest on this trip and praise the work she and all those who volunteer have done to put this on. I express my outside passion for the sport, and she offers me an opportunity to get involved as a volunteer. For a brief second, I contemplate saying yes, and then remind myself of the realities of my life back home—my job, my bills, my responsibilities—and sadly decline. Perhaps some other time I tell her, but I know opportunities rarely, if ever, present themselves twice.

As I walk away deep in thought, I push down the longing to follow my own passions in this manner and try to stay present rather than sinking into the deep self-pity I often feel over my current life scenario. A few hundred yards away from the dancing and chatting main crowd, I find a few US comrades sitting on a blanket with a group of Russians. As I walk over, I recognize a young girl who has been on-site all week from the local university as a translator. I am welcomed by the group with big smiles and a shot of vodka—the first of many to come. The group is made up of her and her husband and their friends. Yes, she is married, at scarcely twenty, and seemingly happy and stable. What a far cry from my own life; yet, I remind myself looks can be deceiving.

They have laid out a traditional Russian picnic of bread, cheese, and salty fish with a texture like sushi, and of course vodka. The group is loud and happy. We drink and toast and take funny photographs, all with the help of our young and quite beautiful translator. It is the epitome of Russian hospitality, and we are reveling in it. How strange a culture that can be so cold and aloof can also be so warm and welcoming.

Our last day in this country we spend in Moscow wandering the streets, admiring the beauty of the landscape. After the long drive into the city, we began our day with lunch in the basement of a Tibet restaurant where we relish the rare occasion of air conditioning. The food was fantastic, a blend of Thai and Tibetan. We took our time and ate slowly, trying many different options and sharing heartily as a group. It was a long overdue relief after days in small-town Kolomna.

A Subway at Midnight

Our group is comprised of two Aussies, a Frenchman, a Welsh girl, and three Americans—all hosted by what is seemingly a guardian angel of a guide. A cousin to one of the Aussie's work colleagues, this brave young woman from a small town in Maryland, intertwines bits of history with her own personal stories of life here in Moscow over the last four years. She tells us about the registration process and the economy and the rituals of life in this once repressed country. As we walk from sight to sight, she recalls her most fearful moment when corrupt and drunk police forced their way into her apartment, guns flailing, tying up her and her boyfriend until their demands for money were met.

We spent the afternoon on a cobblestone street lined with shops for both tourists and locals alike. Down an alley, I notice a gathering of approximately 100 people with picket signs, chanting loudly. They are surrounded by armed men in black uniforms who I correctly assume are police. I look to our host to translate, and she explains it's a labor rally of a well-known anti-government group. Just then, there is a loud commotion down the street. As I turn, I hear people screaming and watch our host's face turn white.

"Run!" she screams to our stunned faces. "Get inside the shops."

Doing as we are told, we make our way into the closest open shop door. It's a porcelain shop filled with endless glass shelves of tiny breakables. The shop owner seems to know this routine, locking the door behind us. And then we wait. Without our translator, we are helpless for an explanation. As we peer out the shop windows, we see military police in riot gear begin surrounding the crowd. Over the next hour, we watch as the protestors are gathered and placed into military vans.

When the last van drives away, the shop owner unlocks the door and motions for us that it is safe to leave. Our group regathers, a combination of curiosity and nerves abound. Our host explain that unlike in America, when these rallies change hands from local police to military police, it is often an excuse to round up anyone in sight, regardless of their actual connection to the event. It is therefore safer to take shelter than risk being on the street. We breathe a collective sigh and continue our exploration of the city. Within moments, we put the incident out of our conversation but not out of our minds.

We wind our way through Red Square, past St. Basil's Cathedral, watch the changing of the guard, enjoy the Alexander Gardens, and visit the Christ Church. In the gardens at 6:00 p.m. sharp, we witness a small band set up and begin to play. There are perhaps thirty band members playing 1940s-style dancehall music as veterans and their lovely partners dance in the open air. They are smiling ever so slightly as they gracefully make their way around the makeshift dance floor, and for just a moment, you could have been anywhere in the world. In a country where smiling at a stranger will have them perceive you as clinically insane, this brief moment allowed a levity of human spirit to show through and it was beautiful.

After what seemed like miles of walking from sight to ever more interesting sight, we settle into dinner at an Indian restaurant two floors above a bustling main thoroughfare. The walls are covered in small tree trunks and exposed wooden beams. There is a couch along one side of the heavy, wood table with a soft, black, velvet cushion. On the other side are chairs resembling King Arthur's throne. We again order a variety of flavors and textures and share with great openness among this international group of friends. We round off the meal with espressos and grape- and mint- flavored hookah.

It is nearly 11:30 p.m. as we leave the restaurant, and there is still one more sight left to see—the metro. Our fearless guide hushes us with the words "No English" as we walk speedily past an enormous number of police. We have already been warned to never look a Russian policeman in the face and to carry only a copy of our visa and passport with us at all times. This particular group, in its large size and at this late hour, does cause my stomach to drop in nervous fear of this unknown phenomenon. As the daughter of a police officer and an American in general, the idea that those in uniform could do more harm than good ignites a very different kind of fear inside me.

A few minutes later, as she purchases our train tickets, the group of officers come filing past us, one by one. I huddle close to the group, silent and looking at the ground. They pass with not a word. Once down in the station, she explains that these are "baby cops," young men who did too poorly on entrance exams for university yet are looking for a path outside of the military. They patrol the metro only and are not allowed to carry guns, only batons. She laughs and assures us they are harmless. I am not as comforted by this as I should be.

We take the circle line from station to station encountering a few locals. One pair of young men who follow us for a while make snide comments in Russian to which our guide both steers us onto a different train and then politely translates for us a version that I am sure is more politically correct than the real one. At another station, a pair of drunk teens run up excitedly applauding the Chelsea futbol team and assuring us they are great fans. She laughs and explains that it must be a match night and that many in Moscow have fallen in love with the Chelsea team since it was purchased by a Russian.

The stations are beautiful, but I am too afraid to take out my camera and draw further attention to the fact we are so blatantly tourists in this unfriendly land. So, the only photos are those of my mind's eye. They are all unique, one with statues and one with mosaics, one with stained glass and one with chandeliers. They are magnificent. Our guide graciously translates plaques on the wall and tells us to rub the dog statue's nose for good luck.

It is late now, and we all are so very tired. We reach our hotel and decide to end the night with one drink at the rooftop bar. The air is crisp, a stark difference from the ever-present heat that has crippled most of Russia this summer. We toast to this amazing day, to our guide, to our friendship, and to our adventure.

I would never see any of the amazing Russian people again. And I will never again step foot on Russian soil either. As this chapter was written, the invasion of Ukraine by Russian forces raged. I could not help but think of the people I met. Are they in support based on brainwashing and propaganda of the Russian government? Or do they see Russia as deserving of this selfish act of violence? Are they silently condemning, or are they part of the thousands who protested and were subsequently punished? One more thing I will simply never know.

Sadly, I would never again see any of those American and international friends either. Soon after this trip, the man I was dating would unknowingly make a critical mistake in our relationship by making plans for an engagement ring. The rumor of this impending marriage proposal would send me straight into a tailspin. Exiting stage right as quickly as possible, I ran, leaving the carnage of a broken-hearted man in my wake. Marriage and the safety and security it represented were the equivalent to suburbs and stagnation. A chapter of life coveted by some, embraced by many. In that moment, I was neither the some nor the many.

Lucky Pile of Tires

"OH MY GOD!" "Jump out!" "Stop the van!"

These statements accompanied by a chorus of screams rang deafening in my ears.

Our van had made a bathroom stop at a small public water stand on the side of a switchback mountain road. Without emergency brakes, the van driver placed a midsized stone under the front wheel to lock it in place on the downhill slope. Desiring snacks from our packs in the rear, the van driver opened the rear door before stepping aside to let us in. As the last person completed her bag rummaging, she slammed the hatch door closed. Suddenly, we watched in horror as the van tire crushed the stone and began to roll toward the cliff's edge.

In an Olympic-worthy acrobatic move, the van driver dove through the open side slider door and into the driver's seat in time to turn the wheel hard to the right, careening it toward an elementary school. We held our breath as the van driver expertly avoided the school and drove directly into an electric pole surrounded by a five-foot-high pile of tires. The van crashed hard against the tires, yet to our amazement, simply bounced backward. A quick check of the engine and we are back on the road, jittery but unscathed.

We ride along in near silence. It is nearly unfathomable the series of perfect timing coincidences that has just saved our belongings, our trip, and potentially children's lives. What if the van driver had not been close by, as quick thinking, or as athletic? What if there was no pile of tires surrounding that electric light pole? It is in moments such as these that we are reminded just how much life can be altered in a split second.

The Ramechhap airport is a single building, less than 1,000 square feet. It is not open to the public except as a pass-through point for luggage checks just before your flight. Visitors stand outside in the dirt field or sit on the nearby rock wall to await the call to board. There is one vendor set up under a blue tarp tent selling sodas, water, chips, and of course, dal bhat.

Upon arrival, we see approximately fifty people waiting to board planes holding just under twenty people each. It is midday by this point, and the sun is hot in this high desert region. Despite the van pandemonium and delay, it appears we will make our flight time. A few break off for drinks and snacks while others walk to stand along the fence line. I am amazed by the seeming chaos of the process and yet somehow it is working.

Then came the loud popping noise reverberating through the valley followed by a small airplane skidding belly first down the runway. With sparks flying, the pilot manages to bring it into a horizontal spin that keeps it from staggering off the runway and into a tall, barbed wire fence. The crowd is deadly quiet, and then erupts in cheers as the pilot waves his hand out the window to signal everyone is OK. We later learn that an unexpected wind gust pushed the plane down, causing the landing gear to be caught on the barbed wire fence on the entry side of the runway, pushing it backward into its storage position and popping the tire.

Plane crashes in Nepal require government inspection before they can be moved from their original location. With officials more than four hours away and the plane directly mid-runway, we were in for a long wait before any departure. We passed the time taking cat naps under nearby shade trees, coercing the roaming goats to eat from our hand, snacking on far too many bags of chips, and of course, recapping the day's events. A lively debate ensued between those believing this much chaos on the first official trekking day meant we were in for a roller coaster and those believing we had gotten chaos out of the way early so the remaining trip would be smooth. In the end, they were both correct. After nearly six additional hours of waiting, an announcement boomed from the airport loudspeaker in Nepalese. Government officials had arrived but deemed their analysis would last beyond dusk. As no flights go into Lukla in the dark, this meant all remaining flights were canceled for the day.

With nowhere to go, we find scant accommodations at a nearby multilevel shack and are served the Nepalese version of takeout. We settle in for the night to watch a rainstorm roll in over the mountain. As I reflect on the chaos of the day, I laugh at the irony. I am partially on this trek to release the chaos of the life I left 8,000 miles away. Just like the trip to Russia and many other places, there is no amount of distance that can eliminate the unexpected.

Someone once enlightened me to a symbolic reality that I have held close for decades: the only way to make murky water turn clear is to stop stirring.

In her book *Thrive: The Third Metric to Redefining Success and Creating a Life of Well-Being, Wisdom, and Wonder* Arianna Huffington, points out that modern society has a tendency to move at such a frenetic pace, we barely recognize life without chaos. We wear stress and overwhelm like a badge of honor and see fully living as frivolous and lazy rather than a luxury to be sought after.

Some years ago, after my second divorce, I vowed to myself to live differently from this societal norm. To value calm, to prioritize self-care, to rise above drama, to change the trajectory of chaos that had ruled my life for so many years. As I watched the rain make its way across the valley that night, I questioned how well I had done. And wondered what I was still in search of. Perhaps, I simply love the mystery hidden in murky water.

Chapter 5:
Lukla & Phakding

Altitude: 2,860m/9,383ft
Travel Time: Five to six hour walk
Soundtrack: If I was a Cowboy, Miranda Lambert

We are awakened before dawn to make our way back to the airfield and attempt to fly out this morning and salvage our trek timeline. The sunrise view from the now familiar rock wall waiting area was nothing short of spectacular. Today's wait was just under three hours. Once we were finally boarded, on this tiny twelve- person plane, we were officially headed into the mountain.

Tenzin-Hillary Airport in Lukla, Nepal, is considered the most dangerous airport in the world. Flanked by high mountain peaks on all sides, the extremely short runway is combined with severely reduced air resistance making it more challenging to slow the plane down. Lukla is a small town in the Khumbu Pasanglhamu rural municipality of the Solukhumbu District in the Province No. 1 of northeastern Nepal.

Despite the adrenaline rush of danger, the flight was one of the most beautiful of my life. The small plane flew so close to the mountain you felt you could reach out and touch the treetops. As our wheels touched down, I let out a sigh surprising myself as I had not realized I was holding my breath. As we gathered our luggage from the plane, I stopped and, in that moment, lost my breath again. Looking around as the sun glinted off the mountains, the sheer majesty of the scenery began to take shape. I am reminded of the last time nature took my breath away so distinctly.

Eiffel Tower in a Red Dress

Unicorn tears. This is how we jokingly began referring to the crystal blue and green hues in the Ligurian and Tyrrhenian Seas surrounding Corsica. The stones from the beach feel smooth as I rub them between my fingers. It's the final day of this eight-day yoga-tourism trip, and I continue to be humbled by the experience of generosity. A stark difference from the frenetic chaos of how it began.

Eight days earlier, I sat alone in the Orlando airport in a panic. With my flight canceled and no easy way to get home to Tampa for the evening, I was desperately working with the airline counter for a rebooking.

Fast forward twelve more hours. I made my way to Heathrow, only to find out my next leg was delayed, and I would be held up in Paris for the night. The good news, I adore Paris and the idea of a bonus night alone in the city was thrilling. The bad news, I would have absolutely none of my luggage. That advice they give you about packing one night of clothing for international trips, take it! Or pack light enough to not check a bag at all.

Dusk was settling over the city as I made my way out of Charles de Gaulle and into the heart of downtown. While in Heathrow, I had gathered the basics of toiletries and makeup from the duty free but clothing was still necessary. Once checked into my hotel, I gathered my best broken French to ask for both a lingerie and a dress shop nearby. Why bother with practicality on an adventure of this magnitude?

The Paris cobblestones were bustling with evening activity, but once I spotted it, you could have heard a pin drop in my mind. A red dress, perfectly framed by the antique architecture of the building window. The waning sunlight glistened off the necklace that accompanied it. I was a virtual moth to a flame.

What transpired next would alter the way I feel about shopping for a lifetime. As a rule, I am not much for shopping. As a petite, in shape woman, I do enjoy being stylish, and I do not carry any particular bodyshame. However, I prefer a minimalist life so outside of vacation remembrances or worked-required basics, I tend to avoid the frivolities of traditional American shopping.

But on this day, I was nothing short of Cinderella. Explaining my luggage plight coupled with adoration for the famed red dress, the sales women were all aflutter to recreate me as a Parisian for the night. Dress, heels, belt, bag, jewelry, and lingerie; I was transformed before their eyes, not just physically but energetically. I could not only feel the hours of travel wash away but also the years of standing in the background, hoping to remain unnoticed. On this night, something shifted.

It wasn't about the dress. It was about what the dress represented. It was independence and empowerment. It was "I've got this" and "I own this" and "I can do this." It was the full belief that no matter what, I could make it on my own. And it was intoxicating.

To witness the tenacity with which I strolled those cobblestone streets, one could have been convinced I was a movie star, rather than a small-town American girl. Making my way to an outdoor café, I mustered all my French skills to order every delectable I love: cheese and bread, escargot, and champagne. And then, my phone dinged.

A colleague had seen my post about being stranded in Paris and realized a mutual friend was also in the city. Two hours later, I was swapping travel stories in an Irish pub with Megan, a friend and colleague from Minnesota. Megan, a technology sales executive and blooming solopreneur abstract artist, embodies every aspect of my ideal self-concept. She is sultry yet feminine, powerful yet whimsical, independent yet approachable. Watching her build her art empire has been a pleasure beyond articulation. There could not have been a more perfect companion to run into halfway around the world that night.

Before dawn the following morning, I was in a cab headed to the airport. Once in Corsica, I spent the next seven days surrounded by sun, sand, friendship, self-reflection, yoga, and laughter . . . endless laughter. There was only one thing the trip lacked: my luggage. Lost in a sea of bureaucracy, my luggage remained lost for the full duration of the trip. Ironically, this would serve as the ying and yang to my feeling of independence from Paris.

A small island, Corsica's shopping is limited to tourist trinkets and the occasional island apparel. Fortunately, my retreat community sprang into action. I was able to amass a bathing suit and two coverups to accompany my red dress and travel clothes. From there, the group took turns "dressing Mel," each sharing at least one of their packed items for my makeshift wardrobe. From yoga pants and sundresses for daylight to shoulder wraps, flowing pants, and jewelry for evenings, I have never felt more beautiful. Cloaked by their clothing, I was also wrapped in their love.

As I ran my fingers along the smooth rocks from the beach, I marveled in gratitude at the juxtaposition of this trip's dynamics. A red dress, an unplanned meeting, a gathering of clothing; the little things that were in fact the big things.

After a quick lunch stop in Lukla, we head toward Phakding, a five to six hour trek away. On our way, we observed beautiful stone walls, painted and non-painted mani stones, a view of Kusum Khangkaru mountain. Phakding is the first viewpoint of Kongde Ri mountain range. It is also home to 500-year-old Pema Choling Monastery.

During this first trek, we pass over a series of swinging cable bridges. My stomach churns and my eyes blur as a fear of heights begins to take hold, and I fall to the back of the group. Taking deep, yogic breaths, I remind myself that thousands of people and hundreds of heavy yaks cross this bridge every day. Trembling, I begin putting one foot in front of the other, white knuckles on the metal cables at my side. I let out yet another exaggerated sigh as I reach the solid ground on the other side. I sit for a moment and think about the gravity of what just transpired. If indeed fear is a cage we build around ourselves, I had just unlocked the first of this adventure. Only there were sure to be hundreds more ahead.

There are dozens upon dozens of books written about these great mountains. Whether drawn to the physicality of the journey or mysticism of the destination, there is a palpable energy about the

Himalaya Mountains that can't be denied.

> *Mountains have always been a place for lowlanders to exercise their imaginations. The abode of snow has offered a vast white screen on which to project fantasies of all comers; exiled kings, foreign imperialists, spiritual seekers, self-important explorers, archaeologists, missionaries, spies, mapmakers, artists, hippies— and climbers.*

> Ed Douglas,
> *Himalaya: A Human History*

There is something about the history of these peaks that feel communal. While my journey is my own, I am not alone in my use of the mountain for spiritual healing and growth. And there is unexplainable comfort in that.

Salman Rushdie has described the Himalayas as "land's attempt to metamorphose into sky." The Tibetans called it Chomolungma (often translated as "Mother Goddess of the World;" for the Nepalis, it was Sagarmatha—"Peak of Heaven"). The head of the surveying operation instead named it Mount Everest, after his retired predecessor George Everest, who was by this time back in England and never set eyes on the mountain that bears his name.

The mountains became stages for mystical self-discovery and Nietzschean improvement. Francis Younghusband, the British explorer, author, and spy, wrote that the Himalayas offered an opportunity for "evolving from ourselves into beings of a higher order."

This first day of trekking is a reckoning. The steep inclines and rough terrain began to distinctly break the group into the highly skilled and overtly challenged. I was pleased to feel my boots wearing comfortably as planned and, with a few adjustments, so was my pack.

Bravado prevailed at a water stop with a push up competition for some, while others used the time to rest and question how much further to town. My legs were aching, but I felt my need for competition pushing me to go faster, to stay with the front of the pack. And yet, we all end in the same place. What is it about our inner competitor that pushes us so fiercely, even at the expense of enjoyment of the present moment?

As we continue the winding path, I find myself alone on the trail. My pace slightly slower than the most agile yet quicker than others. I am fascinated by the intricate black and white graphics carefully painted on the rocks but am left wondering what it says as I am nowhere near our translators. I find this to hold a particular irony. As independent as I claim to be, none of us really thrives alone. It is possible, perhaps, to survive but to really thrive we need the help of those who either walk the path before us or simply help illuminate our circumstance in ways we may not see.

I have been blessed with dozens of close friends and mentors over the years, but three arrived at a particularly critical moment in time. As with the community from Corsica, each came into my life at just the time they were needed. Each helped me grow and thrive personally and professionally. But far more important, each bore witness to a separate but equally venomous situation that I was struggling to get out of. And each, in their own unobtrusive way, found and threw the life preserver I needed to survive.

Human Life Preservers

The day I received the email from Carrie, asking to meet, I could only vaguely remember her face. As my sorority's alumni advisor, she recognized my name as a fellow member from her own home chapter and reached out to meet. And just like that, in our very first meeting, we would begin a friendship as strong as steel, even thru life's ebbs and flows. But the timing of her arrival was no accident—it was pure serendipity.

We were as different as we were similar; a true ying and yang. Both studying for our doctoral degrees, one floor above the other in the same building; she was brilliant at stats and numbers while I excelled with words. She would go on to pursue a more traditional academic career. I would take a winding path in and out of academia. Her energy could capture a room, while I was often the quiet observer.

She gave birth to a beautiful baby boy, while I remained childless. But our intuition was a match to be reckoned with. It would often seem we could read each other's minds, or just instantaneously sense what we might be feeling. We believed in the same human values, laughed at the same style of humor, and indulged in the same frivolity and mischief. Some days we even wore the same outfit without discussion. Most important, we were each other's lifeline.

From an hour-long gossip session in a dance club bathroom on my thirtieth birthday to a seven-hour tear-filled car ride to the mountains while her heart was breaking. From a one-time-only New Year's adventure gone awkwardly awry, to our standing Thursday Game Night picnic style on my living room floor. We were there through mutual divorces, messy breakups, and career disappointments. I was in Miami for her surprise engagement and she was in Colorado for my clock tower wedding extravaganza. And when I was at my darkest point, she was there to answer my two a.m. call.

Me: "Carrie, I am scared."

Her: "Can you go somewhere safe for the night? I can leave now and be there by 7:00 a.m."

Me: "I can't ask you do to that."

Her: "You can't ask me not to."

As the years moved on, our life's symmetry waned. I stayed single and childless, focused solely on career and travel. She remarried and added three additional children to her career mom super-status. They bought second properties; I started second companies. But we remain each other's cheerleader from afar. Like so many moments of life, the length of time we were closely intertwined proved inconsequential. What mattered was the timing and vulnerability of our friendship. The right mix, at the right time, became the right lifeline.

"You must dig the trenches, then the water will flow."

Bob O'Leary

The humblest man I have ever known, Robert O'Leary, is a tower of wisdom, experience, and grace. A Georgetown graduate, he began his career working on Capitol Hill on initiatives of societal importance like supporting the work of the National Organization for Women and the Equal Rights Amendment. Back in his home state of Michigan, he was the chief deputy director of the Commerce Department and later served as Governor Blanchard's deputy chief of staff and the president of the Michigan Accident Fund. Recruited to Florida by Governor Lawton Chiles, his humility and authenticity made him a masterful change agent and the reinvention and restructuring guru of the Executive Staff. He was responsible for closing the Commerce Department, restructuring the Department of Health and Rehabilitative Services, creating Enterprise Florida and Workforce Florida, Redesigning the Labor Department, merging the Departments of Administration and General Services into DMS, and much more. But if you were to ask him, he'd simply say he was a guy in a closet office under the stairs.

I met Bob in 2005 on my first day at ICUF. For our introductory first six hours, we sat in the glowing florescent light of the dreary office building on Monroe Street while he painstakingly walked me through the last fifteen years of ICUF policy stances, and I incessantly flipped a highlighter out of boredom and general fidgeting.

As the years ticked by, Bob and I developed a natural rhythm of working together. He was the big idea man; I was the practical implementation specialist. He would boldly devise plans well ahead of their time, and I would work tirelessly to translate those plans into a language to gain buy-in. He would think nothing of it if it were ignored while I would reel from perceived rejection. He would impart knowledge, and I would eagerly push the envelope. He would humbly push all the credit my way while we both knew I could never have completed the project without his guidance. His presence in my life loomed large both at work and in the chaos of my second marriage. I never felt judged, even when I failed, no matter which arena. We simply assessed the damage, gathered the lessons to be learned, and focused on the next move.

As a big-picture thinker and future-focused leader, Bob was always ahead of the curve. He conceived problems and their subsequent solutions before others even sounded the alarm. His words and actions provided a powerful example of forging through doubtful voices of others and instead remaining steadfast toward the greater good ahead. Throughout my career, I have harkened back to this sentiment often. Work hard for what you believe in, even when no one appreciates it. They will eventually. Leaders often must perform the hard work of digging the trenches of new ideas, processes, or paths so that others may follow. In the end, if your desire is to leave this world a better place, then you dig, not with resentment of the extra work but with great exhilaration and pride, for you alone can later stand on the bank and revel in the water that flows behind.

While we stayed in touch after I moved from Tallahassee to Tampa, a decade later I still mourn the loss of our daily interaction. The six years we worked directly together did as much to mold my perception of life as any other chapter. He taught me to be steadfast but humble, to be fearless but grounded, to believe in what is possible—even if no one else does.

"You can't set yourself on fire to keep others warm."

Dr. Fred Seamon

There is a distinct shift in the energy of the room when Dr. Fred Seamon walks in. It is unclear if it is his mile-wide smile or the warmth in which he greets everyone he meets like an old friend. Either way, Fred is a legend to anyone who has the pleasure of knowing him.

He began his career in late 1960s in the juvenile court system, and over fifty years later, he is still fighting for equality and diversity. While on the graduate faculty at Florida State University (FSU) and at the Pepper Institute on Aging, he conducted several major research studies related to diversity, equity, and inclusion in public employment and social and economic disparities among minority elderly populations. His experience includes providing diversity training to law enforcement personnel via the Florida Department of Law Enforcement Senior Leadership Program, the Florida Department of Highway Safety Management Fellows Program, and the Department of Insurance Executive Institute. He was recently an invited participant in the White House Conference Call for African American Stakeholders on COVID- 19 and the CARES Act, April 2020.

Fred and I first crossed paths in 2002 when I arrived in Tallahassee as a bubbly doctoral student at Florida State. Active in the campus and broader community, his reputation of kindness-driven leadership proceeded him. However, it was more than a decade later that his impact on my life truly began. In 2018, I joined the consulting firm where he was a legacy employee. While the firm turned into a wilder ride than either of us ever imagined, Fred's steady guidance was a constant calm I desperately needed. Even after I left the firm, his regular check-ins would bring a smile to my heart knowing I was cared for and cheered on.

All of Fred's accomplishments pale in comparison to the living, breathing example of leadership he is as a man. He is the first to say yes to any opportunity that will add value to those he cares for, be that his family, company, community, or church. He will never ask of you what he will not do himself. He is the cheerful rally to a team that is down. He is the insightful influencer in times of controversy. And he is a voice of reason during times of distress.

Upon seeking his steady council for a decision weighing heavy on my heart, he was all too willing to put aside his busy schedule to listen, comfort, and reflect. The lessons he shared were powerful reminders. Be confident in the value you add. Set and keep limits on what you can healthily give of yourself. Be willing to walk away from what doesn't serve you. There is always another door to open.

Lonesome Dove

> *Rippling is the way in which each of us, often without being conscious or cognizant of doing so, creates concentric circles of influence that affect others.*
>
> Dr. Irvin Yalom,
> *Staring at the Sun*, pg. 192

At each of life's crossroads, I found people who were living embodiments of the best of humanity. Their lessons of love, humility, perseverance, and self-empowerment have truly shaped the woman I am today. And yet there are likely so many more. They helped me see my own inadequacies in a way that inspired me to change rather than retreat to defensiveness. And from that place I could grow.

Some fear loneliness and mold their lives to ensure they are always surrounded by others. For me, being let down by others chipped away at the trust I held for community. It also began to make commitment look like claustrophobia. Especially the idea of motherhood. Perhaps this is why I never fought harder for that dream.

> *Contemplating the result of the pregnancy test, I envisioned myself on a train lugging a baby, a computer, books, and the requisite ton of baby paraphernalia and I couldn't imagine how I would*

103

> *carry all that stuff.*
>
> *I realize, looking back, that the image of myself struggling on the train with too much baggage was analogous to my sense of what being a mother would feel like: weighted down, immobilized.*
>
> *I learned to pack light and not carp about delays. I like having the kind of life where you didn't know what was going to come next; the opposite of what life as a mother would be, or so I presumed.*
>
> Laura Kipnis,
> *Maternal Instincts*, pg. 37

If, like me, we have an independent spirit, we may begin to circle the wagons believing doing it all ourselves, carrying it all alone, is better than the disappointment of rejection. But the universe has a way of reminding us that we simply can't carry it all, all the time. On an island off the coast of France, that lesson rang out loud and clear. Through the steadfast guidance of two life-changing mentors and the unwavering support of a life-long friend, I was reminded again and again.

As I turned the corner toward Phakding, my eyes are met with the red, blue, and yellow of the buildings and the sounds of a bustling village. It's a stark contrast to the quiet solitude of the trail, and I welcome it. In the distance I can see my group beginning to huddle together, and I quicken my pace to join them. That night in Phakding, we toasted a glass of ginger tea to the first day of hard trekking behind us and the adventure that lie ahead. I took a sip, letting the bite of the ginger linger on my tastebuds.

Years later, I would purchase Megan's painting inspired by that night in Paris and hang it prominently in my foyer. A constant reminder of the beautiful intertwine between independence and community. We can never really control where life will lead, but if you put the right people around you, you can be assured you will survive. I may enjoy my lonesome dove heart but perhaps, experiences like these, remind me I also do not have to remain a tumbleweed for life.

Chapter 6:
Namche Bazaar

Altitude: 3,440m/11,286ft
Travel Time: Seven to eight hour walk
Soundtrack: Paradise City, Guns N' Roses

From Phakding, we walk toward Namche Bazaar, passing both the Rimshung and Uchhecholing Monasteries. We climb up along the trail and visit Sagarmatha National Park where we have our first glimpse of Mount Everest.

As we round the corner, the city comes into sight for the first time. Embedded on the hillside, its multiple levels spring alive with bright colors and bustling streets.

Namche Bazaar is a town in Khumbu Pasanglhamu Rural Municipality in Solukhumbu District of Province No. 1 of northeastern Nepal. It is located within the Khumbu area at 3,440 meters at its lowpoint, populating the sides of a hill. Most Sherpa who are in the tourism business are from the Namche area.

Namche serves as the main gateway to Everest, and the most colorful of the Khumbu region villages. It houses modern shops like North Face with high-end hiking gear directly across from rustic Tibetan markets where traditional garments and tourist T-shirts intertwine.

Namche Bazaar is unsurprisingly popular with trekkers in the Khumbu region. There are German bakeries, little cafés, many restaurants, and a beauty salon. There is also an Irish pub, considered to be the most remote in the world. Namche is the main trading center and hub for the Khumbu region with many Nepalese officials, police check post, and a bank. It is hard to believe this thriving, modern village is in the middle of a mountain range, accessible only by yak, foot, or emergency helicopter.

The group enters Namche in phases, gathering as we arrive in a bakery and café with a picnic area and outdoor seating complete with lifelike Astroturf. I indulge in a caprese salad followed by the chocolate croissant. It is the first fresh food I have had in four days and will be the last for many more. Like most countries in the region, tourists are advised to eat only cooked meals. Today I take my chances, and it does not disappoint.

Once we are all gathered, we are led to our tea house. By far the most elaborate since Kathmandu with private showers and hot water. We unpack and reorganize in preparation for the coming days, knowing this is the last stop for any needed supplies.

Randy chooses a nap over exploration, so I head out alone. The winding streets are filled with makeshift market tents in front of brick and-mortar shops. The air is filled with a mixture of burning incense and the ever-present dal bhat with the occasional waft of mountain freshness. I stroll past cheap trinkets and handmade leather items. Knowing I should add nothing to my pack at this point in the trek, I opt for a quiet coffee shop, an espresso, and a comfy seat with a view. Pulling out my journal, I struggle to adequately capture the scene around me and instead stare off toward the mountains, lost in thought.

Four Quarters of Utopia

There is endless nostalgia wrapped into the energy of a physical place. We attach memories and emotions to the sights, smells and energy of the places that become embedded in our soul. Namche Bazaar is a little village of pure Nepalese utopia in the midst of a vast unknown. Not unlike this Nepalese mountainside village, the utopias of real life hold both beauty and ugly, joy and pain.

Anyone who has a life chapter they call their "wild days" has their version of a place that reminds them of that chapter. It isn't the actual place that matters, but rather who we were in that place that is usually bittersweet. For me, this was a chapter wrapped in my love of football.

Football was a part of my soul since infancy. At my University, football, and the accompanying tailgates, were the stuff of legends. Fall Saturdays will forever represent my wild chapter, filled with so much laughter and fun but nearly overshadowed by the burden of poor choices and the longing for the unattainable. Equal parts masked and fueled by an endless flow of alcohol. Utopia, after all, is an imagined place or state of things in which everything is perfect, making it completely unattainable. And yet, I spent years searching for it.

It's Saturday morning, and I am awake at dawn with anticipatory butterflies circling in my stomach. A run, a bagel, and a carefully crafted outfit selection all lie ahead before the magic entry time.

Tallahassee is a city with three seasons: football, legislative, and summer. And the weather is hot for two of three. Game days hold ritualistic traditions that are nearly clockwork in their routines. And the pageantry of preparation is at an all-time high.

The days represent a full festival repeated a half dozen times a year. Hours before kickoff, we begin making our rounds through the tailgates. Elaborate displays of cult-like team obsession with feasts for a king and parking lot TVs larger than in living rooms. A who's who of the town, you circle to see and be seen. And then we descend.

With a Willy Wonka-style precious golden ticket, a few times a year you could enter this magical place—the privileged football skybox. It was a college football bubble where time and space stood still. Equally representing the have and have nots, it was also a level playground for all forms of mischief. A place where once inside, wealth, status, age, and prominence went out the window. A place where you were giddy with anticipation of the garb to be worn and the new acquaintances to be met. In this place, for six to eight hours at a time, the outside world was nonexistent. The struggles, fears, questions, and misgivings all melted away into dancing, drinking, and frivolity. In this magical world, societal norms were given a proverbial middle finger—something to worry about another day. We revel in the sounds of Gene and the tastes of Jack. We turned stairs and railings into dance floors. We broke bottles and ceiling tiles. We looked out through the broad windows and pretended they are the windows on the entire world instead of our one tiny slice.

This utopia was garnet and gold colored Kool-Aid, the best and worst kind of drug. A drug you can't shake. Where the hits had to be more frequent, the stunts more outlandish, the emotions more volatile. Where the hangover, literal and figurative, became increasingly intolerable, and yet you never voluntarily said no. We were fast friends, our own universe, sharing a secret elixir. The antidote to a loneliness no one acknowledged.

We were an unlikely band as different as we were alike. Different reasons for being called by utopia. Requiring different doses of the drug to feel whole. Different worlds we indulged to escape. But we were all searching, all coping, all running from something. Broken marriages, lapsing careers, mental health challenges, imposter syndromes, failures, and burdensome expectations—the 100-pound weights we piled outside the door like shoes outside a Buddhist temple. Only to begrudgingly retrieve them hours later. All who entered found release and escape from what weighed so heavy. There was not one of us who walked lightly. With perfect ease. Is there ever?

Utopia is, of course, a myth. A temporary belief as false as flat earth. As with all states of imagination, reality will reveal itself when the fog clears. For every laugh served by this utopia was an equal sized crack in life's permanent realities. For every Sunday morning inside joke, gossip raged, egos were wounded, insecurities were heightened, and relationships were damaged. And yet, we loved every, single, moment of it.

Shame Monster

When you dig into the past in a real, raw way—what I call excavating the attic of your life choices—you have to be prepared to sit in the discomfort of what you uncover. And my attic was a virtual torture chamber. Full of poor decisions with ugly consequences. And yet I knew to move beyond them, I had to face them, own them, understand them, and eventually grow from them. And so it began.

Heidi Stevens, Soulful business coach, talks about the dark parts of our soul gathering on a bus and taking turns driving.

> *And so to notice that when fear starts coming up and driving the bus or when ego-based thoughts that want to keep us locked in—fear, shame, guilt, unworthiness—when those start coming up and we know them because they don't feel good in our body. They feel like a black hole, they start taking us down.*

> *It's not about alienating them or trying to eradicate them. It's actually about naming them, seeing them, and genuinely asking them to take a back seat in the bus. Fear I see you. I hear you. I'm going to hold you right here and I'm also going to ask you to take a back seat.*

I was a mean drunk. Full stop. For years, drinking with me was a journey which began with me peeking out of my introverted shell to become that giggly life of the party girl who sings at the top of her lungs in a tiara. And it became what could only be described to me the next day as a sight as ugly as the Beast himself.

Drinking stole a lot of my memories. I'm not sure why I can black out mentally so much earlier than physically, or why alcohol rarely made me physically sick, but mentally, I could become a different person in a matter of hours.

At times I am relieved that ignorance is bliss on much of my drunken immaturity. But other times, I struggle to remember meaningful moments with others. Girls' trips to vineyards, beach sunsets with my mom, Ybor strolls with old friends, and perhaps most painful, heartfelt I love yous lost in the black hole of my lapsed memory. Only to find years later while rummaging through old journals, photos, and texts.

Enter Shame Monster.

Monster and I go way back. From one of my first drinks, at a high school party in Whisper Bay, where I stumbled to my car, propped on the hatchback before melting to the ground hoping to sober up before curfew. (P.S. I didn't and by some miracle I made it the two miles home without wrecking, killing myself, or harming anyone else.)

As life went on, Monster and I intertwined spontaneously. At times, I grasped a hold of life so tight that every move kept him at arm's length. Sometimes he was there, but I could keep his taunting at bay, convincing myself he told lies or at least exaggerated. I couldn't possibly have said those things, looked that foolish, or acted that irrational.

Then there were the dark days. The days I'd wake up with Monster in my face, silently shaking his head in disgust. Actions that cost me friendships, damaged relationships, and stifled career growth. It was on these days, I knew deep in my core that I was a better human than this, that my life was in complete misalignment. I knew I could do better.

In high school, I had two distinct sets of best friends. Only one is still in my life today, and I know exactly why. Sydney and I became friends somewhere between elementary and middle school but grew close in high school. A year my senior, she inspired me at every turn. Talented, smart, and confident, she never seemed to need anyone's particular attention. She took hours to get ready for the simplest of activities, which I would publicly bemoan but secretly love as it gave me time to chat with her intellectually intriguing and always encouraging father.

Sydney was an only child and since I spent most of my childhood without a present sibling, we shared the intense comfort of solo activities but relished friends as well. Both drawn to the stage, we spent many nights in rehearsal or backstage of a performance dreaming of our future in New York or LA. By her side I had my first drink, smoked my first joint, and went to my first dive bar—all things that scared me terribly, but her fearlessness was enough for both of us. I could tell her anything and feel like she would respond with her usual calm, rational advice. Neither judging nor condoning, just listening.

The throes of adolescence can often feel as if it is the hardest time of our lives. For me, I can't imagine surviving adolescence without the foundation of her friendship. She was the sister I needed when that deep sense of loneliness crept in at home. She was the person who always saw me and really understood me—or at least tried.

Sydney went off to college a year before me, and I spent as many weekends in her dorm room as I did my own high school bedroom. However, when it came time to select a college for myself, I knew I needed to go down a different path, for fear of never growing wings of my own. Once both away at college, then law school for her and grad school for me, our friendship became increasingly challenging to maintain. Over the years, it drifted to a few calls a year and maybe one face-to-face dinner or happy hour. But in those moments, no matter how much time has passed, it always feels like home. It is a rare circle of safety where Shame Monster is never allowed.

In complete contrast, I stand outside a restaurant window and watch as three lost friendships and Shame Monster share a decades long meal. In my senior year, I formed a bond with three other girls, and we were a quad to be reckoned with. Each unique in her own way—the cheerleader, the dancer, the beautiful girl next door, and me. Although all having other outside friendships, we were virtually inseparable. I assumed we would be the kind of friends that still had girls' trips into our eighties.

But then graduation came, and I spent that summer spiraling through one party after another, each with a silly boy craze to match. I was fully aware my phone had stopped ringing with their invites for sleepovers and girls' nights in, but I pretended not to notice. I rationalized it was inevitable since we were all headed in separate directions for college, and I would never consider moving back to this town. But deep down I was grieving. Deep down I knew it was my own choices that had pushed them away.

By the time everyone left for college, we were barely speaking. It was a time in history where keeping up through distance was not as easy as a text but not impossible with effort. And I am as guilty as anyone for lack thereof.

Over the years, I watched with envy through social media as they continued to deepen their friendship through weddings and careers and babies. I longed to meet their kids or share in their career journeys, but the more time passed, the harder it was to envision a reconnection.

And then came our high school reunions. Our ten-year reunion is a blur of frenzied planning, awkward fake smiles, and carefully navigating my ex's need for constant attention. I knew it would be a mistake to invite him, but of course he insisted, and I relinquished control. Being a part of the planning committee meant I had extra duties to attend to and having already strained high school relationships myself, there was no one all that interested in meeting or interacting with him. His impatience got the best of him, and we left the reunion soon after the first event began.

Ten years later, I was determined to change the narrative. I was happy, single, in great shape, had just taken the position of nonprofit CEO. There was just one problem. I drank. I drank a lot. I used alcohol to lubricate conversation and shield me from rejection and awkwardness. Which, of course, is counter-productive as it only leads to more nights of shame and regret.

The scenes from that weekend were an especially difficult box for me to reopen. With Shame Monster right by my side, chiding me at every artifact, I dug in to face them one by one. There was the night one of those former best friends and her husband generously walked me back to my hotel only to have me rudely chastise them the entire way for "making" me leave the party. There was the awkward sister bonding moment I spoiled when I was alone at the bar having brunch, spotted them and moved my stool to insert myself into their conversation. There was my naivete to allow a childish mean girl scenario to play out as a classmate set me up to be laughed at by the entire group. On the flight home from that weekend, I stewed in my own humiliation.

Perhaps now is a good time to squirrel into a note of sincerity. To the dozen or so friends and family who have seen the "dark days," let me just say thank you and I am sorry. Thank you for the safe walks home, the blind eye to nonsense, the deaf ear to hurtful words. For the hurricane of irrational, angry emotion that spewed out of the crater of my own misalignment. I'd take it all back if I could, but alas time machines have yet to be perfected. But please know, I remember, I own it, and I am sorry.

Shame Monster did not only appear alongside my elixir of choice or in a morning haze, he also appeared with biting snarls when I was overly stressed from work. Or when a loneliness crept in that I could not shake and the need for attention sent me grasping unsuitable partners. But nothing can compare to the shame turned guilt of childlessness.

The Empty Rocking Chair

In the time directly following my hysterectomy, I fell into a deep spiral of guilt about my life as a childless woman. I was mourning the life I had envisioned that never was. I cried at the Christmas Hallmark commercial featuring a young grandma telling the story of the tree's ornaments to an infant while the parents fall asleep on the couch nearby. I put on a thousand brave faces at friends' baby showers and kids' school events. I had fallen in love with children who were not my own and lost them for the same reason. I carried a daily ten-ton weight of guilt for having a mother so perfectly made to be a grandmother and not offering her a grandchild to love and dote upon. What if I had made better life partner choices when I was younger? What if I had drank less and settled down more? What if? What if?

But the truth is, this is exactly where I am supposed to be. For there lies the beauty in the ugliness. The messiness. The sheer disjointedness of the human experience.

So many times, when we are enlightened to the ugliness, we recoil. It is so misaligned with who we long to be, who we claim to be. We want to get as far away from it as possible. We confine the ugly to rice paper

117

journals, or dusty boxes in the far corners of our mind. If we don't speak of it, will there be a time it will be erased? We hope so.

It does make me sad I did not get to experience motherhood and watch my mother be the world's greatest grandmother to my own child. But I had to learn to let go of the guilt associated with that in order to heal. There is no guarantee this body would ever have carried a baby no matter what different choices I made.

In *Selfish, Shallow, and Self-Absorbed: Sixteen Writers on The Decision Not To Have Kids*, Kate Christensen describes her own journey to loving her childless life in a way that has come to resonate with me.

> *We have this life, and we are these people. We get to go to bed every night together, alone, and wake up together, alone. Our shared passions thrill and satisfy us, and our abundant freedoms—to daydream; to cook exactly the food we want when we want it; to drink wine and watch a movie without worrying about who's not yet asleep upstairs; to pick up and go anywhere we want, anytime; to do our work uninterrupted; to shape our own days to our own liking; and to stay connected to each other without feeling fractured—are not things we'd choose to give up for anyone, ever. I attribute my present-day happiness to sheer luck. I didn't choose not to have kids, it just happened to me*

There are simply no guarantees in life at all. Shame and guilt cannot bring healing, no matter how far we push it down or how long we wait. Just the opposite: bringing it all into the light, sitting face-to-face with your whole self, the beautiful and the ugly, the visions and the delusions—this is the only path to freedom.

And so, it happened for me. I pulled out the journals and out poured the dust from broken ceiling tiles and broken promises. Out came the miles from the irrational chase. Out came the what ifs, the one days, the if onlys.

I allowed my soft-spoken self to stare into the eyes of my sharp-tongue self until she too softened. To own the alcohol fueled snakebites that led to a daily Monster sighting. I sat with the discomfort until the urge to hide from it all completely faded. Until utopia was simply another set of footsteps on my life's path. Footsteps to be honored for their power and simultaneous lack thereof.

The sun is just disappearing when I see a few of the group beginning to gather at the Irish pub on the level just below. Walking out to greet them I take one more look around this village in the sky. Perhaps utopia is real after all. But perhaps real utopia is not a state of perfection at all. Perhaps it is instead the acceptance of imperfection—in ourselves, in our choices, and in our attempts to be better each day.

> *Somebody is always going to be disappointed with your*
> *life choice, and my rule of thumb is that as long as I'm*
> *not the one who is disappointed, I can live with that.*

Jen Kirkman,
I Can Barely Take Care of Myself:
Tales From a Happy Life Without Kids, pg. 6

Chapter 7:

Tengboche

Altitude: 3,870m/12,694ft
Travel Time: Five to six hour walk
Soundtrack: ABCDEFU, Gayle

With the Ramechhap airport delay, we are a day behind on our trek, leaving us to skip the extra night in Namche and begin again the following day. Heading toward Tengboche from Namche, we have our first view of Ama Dablam, Lhotse Shar, Taboche, Kangtega, and Thamserku. It is a mountainside tea hut where vendors also display beautiful, beaded bracelets. I purchase one for myself—white beads with brown speckles and a red drawstring. I am not sure why that one called to me specifically, but it became the lasting memory for years after wearing it the entire remaining trek. I also purchased one as a gift to each of my nieces—jade and amethyst beads, respectively. Careful to select one extra small for my nieces' tiny wrists. To me, they represent a piece of this adventure. I long to be an inspiration to them both, and I can only hope they find their own version of Nepal early and often.

After tea, we continue on a nondescript portion of the trail until an army barrack at Phunke Tenga and soon arrive in Tengboche.

Tengboche is a village in Khumbu Pasanglhamu rural municipality in the Khumbu subregion of Province No. 1. It is a midway station on the trail to the base camp for the mountain climbers of Mount Everest and other peaks of over 8,000 meters (26,000 feet) elevation. This entire area of the Khumbu region up to the Tibet border is considered Sagarmatha National Park.

Sagarmatha National Park was established in 1976. In 1979, it became the country's first national park that was inscribed as a Natural World Heritage Site by the United Nations Educational, Scientific and Cultural Organization (UNESCO).

Tengboche is home to an important Buddhist monastery, which is the largest gompa in the Khumbu region. Although the structure was built in 1923, Buddhist tradition in the area is said to date back more than 350 years. The towering structure is made all the more prominent by the desolate landscape surrounding it.

The monastery has been destroyed twice: once by an earthquake, and once by a fire. Each time it was rebuilt by the community with support of foreign aid. The rebuilt monastery was formally consecrated in 1993 and is considered the gateway to Mount Everest. The religious room of the Guru Rimpoche in the monastery was fully restored in September 2008. The entrance gate has also been rebuilt with funds provided by the Greater Himalayas Foundation based in Washington, DC.

We are invited to participate in the evening chanting and prayer sessions, which I am especially eager to do. Despite the excitement of this journey, there is a heavy weight still on my soul. As I sit on the cold, wooden floor awaiting the monks to file into the main room, I close my eyes, say a prayer of gratitude, and ask for guidance and release. Then I allow my mind to listen only to my breath. Before long, the chanting begins. As the sounds become vibrations, I am transported.

A PowerPoint of Lies

The need for control is always based in fear. People in need of control showcase this need in a variety of ways—most often by exploiting fear. The most cunning will find specific triggers and combine those with their own power, a toxic combination of intimidation.

When this happened at twenty-six, in my second marriage, I was crippled by it. Blindsided, I had no idea what was happening to me. When it repeated itself in the workplace years later, it took only one sleepless night to realize what was happening and take back my own power.

The drive along the interstate to the city that morning was filled with traffic and anticipation. I had prepared for weeks for this two-hour meeting, compiling research from sources I trust and those that would impress. I had confident butterflies for the opportunity to shine, proudly showcasing my depth of knowledge.

If I am honest, my gut knew something was amiss. A newly hired executive had done a write up of a few of us, and it had been confidentially shared with me. The write up was kind but also spot-on, and I knew it would send my boss into a tailspin. The report pointed to my authentic need for meaning in my work and estimated I would stay no more than two years without meaningful change with my current role. I knew my boss saw departure from the company as personal betrayal, and it was often followed by verbal retaliation at every turn. What I didn't know was how contorted these words would turn in her mind.

The meeting began cordially, with her listening while I excitedly illustrated my thoughts and plans for the new role. Halfway through, she interrupted me with a backhanded insult, a red flag that made my gut churn, and yet I decided to ignore, carefully navigating the land mines.

No sooner had I completed my presentation, she was trading computers to begin hers. It began with the professional equivalent to "this is for your own good."

"It has come to my attention that you are unhappy and frustrated, and I want to understand it so we can do what we need to do to retain you."

Then came the bomb. A PowerPoint where she meticulously outlined a list of my flaws. Some were stings of truth, others out of context daggers only meant to pierce, and still others complete fabrications. Hours ticked by as she articulated each detail in a swirl of condescension.

"All your peers feel this way."

"You are negative."

"You are aggressive."

"You have conflict with everyone."

"Everything you say is harsh."

"You always assume negative intent."

"All the company gossip begins and ends with you."

"You have no capacity to take feedback."

I sat stunned, taking it all in, before excusing myself to the bathroom to catch my breath. My mind drifted to individual conversations. I do have a harsh tone and curt demeanor when I am stressed and, in this role, I was always stressed. But I had worked diligently over the last year to gain patience and a softer tone. I do like to have unwavering command over my deliverables but doesn't everyone when you are regularly quizzed for specifics at any given moment. But conflict with everyone? Negative intent? My mind raced. I knew this was not true. I knew my concerns over company culture were vetted with colleagues who not only agreed but often instigated the conversations. I knew I carefully shielded my team and our clients from the negativity and promoted the company to the fullest.

I stared blankly at my own face in the bathroom mirror. There was something eerily similar to the way this conversation was playing out. My mind flashed back to a hard, wooden bench outside a courtroom.

Vindication in a White Binder

Anxiety swirled to the point of nausea. I sat as the minutes ticked by like hours. The February air was cold as it gusted through the large oak hallways, causing shivers each time the heavy exterior doors opened and shut. Or it could simply be nerves.

At long last, my name was called, and we filed in. He sat to the right, accompanied by an entourage: his lawyer, his ex-wife, and his best friend, each glaring at me as they entered. I was directed to the left side, armed only with a large, white binder. I was completely alone, and my soul felt every breath of that.

It was three months since our divorce had been finalized and eight months since he was sent to jail for domestic violence. And yet the drama continued. There seemed to be endless reasons he needed to interact with me. His latest excuse, a demand for me to give him the washer and dryer from the home we once shared. I had foolishly left off the specificity of that item belonging to the house that I obtained during the divorce, and it was now being used as a weapon.

Struggling financially, my first instinct was to reason with him to leave it. He had one at his rental house. It was clear this was out of spite. When that failed, I became indignant about it being part of the house, which only infuriated him back into cycles of harassment. He would call and text day and night, demanding I stop what I was doing and let him come over to get them. By this point his volatility kept me in a place of fear. I didn't want to be alone with him even in public, much less inside my house. But I also feared what he would do to the house should I allow him in without me.

Then on a cold February day, it all came to a head. As my team and I sat in a strategy meeting waiting on a call from our lobbyist, my phone sat face up on the table. The calls and text messages rolled in, frenetically one after another after another. Getting progressively angrier and more aggressive as time went on and they were left unanswered.

Glancing over just as one particular explicative message appeared on the screen, Bob stopped in mid-sentence. I was pale and shaking, trying simultaneously to focus and not cry. He knew what was happening. They all did. I had been harassed at the office so many times they had a restraining order written, ready to file at a moment's notice.

"What is it today?" he inquired with a tone gentler than I was entitled to. After a brief explanation, he concluded the meeting and ushered me to his car.

"Where are we going?"

"To stop this."

We made our way to his house for a rolling dolly and a tarp then to mine where we rolled the washer and dryer to my porch, carefully covered it with a tarp, and headed back to the office. Once safely there, I texted a response to let him know I was done talking about them, and they were ready for him to pick up.

In a rational scenario, this would have ended the event. But this was far from a rational scenario. It wasn't about the washer and dryer. It never was. It was about power. Power of holding something that could keep us intertwined, keep us communicating. Taking that power back from him only increased his volatility.

That night after work, I received a knock at the door. I was served with a temporary protective order. On the order was a completely fabricated story of me stalking him. A false plea that I was a threat to him and the kids. I was shocked. After everything we had been through, this blatant lie was a new kind of gut punch. And the punches were just beginning.

Over the next seven days, while awaiting our day in court, he sent me more than a dozen messages, called half a dozen times, and left flowers and notes on my doorstep. The messages oscillated between love notes of repentance and messages of seeming hysterics; from "this is all a huge misunderstanding" to "I left the oven on, please go over and shut it off."

Luckily by this time, the veil of reality was finally lifted. He was attempting to bait me into responding so I would violate the TPO and he could petition to have me arrested. When no replies from me came, his messages quickly devolved from "I thought you loved me" into angry strings of expletives. Each time I stayed silent but carefully documented. Into the white binder they went.

On the day of the hearing, he presented his false claims to the court. His story of lies was vastly different from what he wrote on the original petition causing a small smile to creep over my face. How flippant of him to not even bother to review the actual lie he created and be able to recount it. The judge, also recognizing the discrepancy, embarked on a series of pointed questions to which he fumbled through. And then at last it was my turn. I refuted his claims, and then offered the binder to the bailiff to give to the judge. Inside, carefully documented with colored tabs and labels, was every part of the truth. A description of the events of the day with a signed affidavit from my mentor. The police filing and sentencing from his previous domestic violence case. And most important, records of each text and call he made to me after filing for the TPO.

The rustle of pages turning was the only sound in that quiet courtroom for what seemed like an eternity. And then, SLAM, the judge violently shut the binder and turned to look directly at him.

For the next five full minutes, the judge proceeded to lecture him on misuse of the court system and his obvious attempt to use this TPO to manipulate and intimidate me. He berated him for being dishonest and reminded him that he was fortunate he was not being charged with perjury.

With every word, my chest swelled with exoneration. It was more than a win; it was a celebration over abuse and manipulation. It was vindication. Hot tears of relief welled up and trickled down my cheeks. I glanced back at his entourage, who were now looking sheepish and gathering their things to leave.

I have never forgotten that feeling, and likely never will. At that moment, I took back the power. I took back ownership of my own life.

Circling the Drain

My focus returned to the mirror in front of me. Taking a deep breath, I gathered my thoughts. Time to hold that feeling close; keep my power. Making my way back to the boardroom, I braced for impact.

"Do you think I am a good CEO? I'm not crazy. I have reasons behind my actions. I have a plan."

Wait. Full stop. Is the CEO of my company defending her own competence? What is happening in her mind to be compelled to do this? Each time I spoke, even to answer a question she specifically posed, I was interrupted, and my comments were discarded. I was scolded for being "defensive." When asked to give reasons behind the stories she brought forth, I could not. How could I? They were twisted realities or untruths.

"I don't understand why you don't communicate with me more," she said. "All your peers meet with me regularly. Why not you? I want us to have a better relationship."

I stared at her blankly. This is your attempt at bettering our relationship?! By this point we were six hours and twenty-two minutes into a two-hour meeting. It was late afternoon, and I had not eaten. I was becoming completely numb to this and ready to just go home.

"I feel like you are incongruent."

And suddenly, I was snapped back to the present. Did she just use my word against me? I saw red. How. Dare. You. A woman who has no capacity to take interest in the humanity of others unless it directly serves her. A woman who has been gaslighting me for the last four hours. It was, of course, just a word. But I knew it was more than that. It was MY word. It was the title of my book and the representation of my deeply personal self-journey. A journey she knew nothing about, only that I was writing a book by that name. Hot tears welled up in my eyes as I seethed in silence.

Four hours later, I nearly stumbled out of the conference room and down the elevator. I was numb. I collapsed on the bench outside the building and called my lifeline. I could barely speak. My voice was breaking, attempting to hold back tears. This day was dehumanizing, demoralizing, and humiliating. My chest throbbed from the emotions.

Alone in the car on the hour drive home, fifteen hours after the day began, a volcano of fury erupted, interspersed by hot tears. I was thankful for the dark of night to hide from other drivers. Once home, I stood in the shower wondering why the tears wouldn't cease. Half of me asking what was I even feeling, the other half self-comforting, allowing space to feel without judgment. I crawled into bed emotionally exhausted yet tossed and turned through tears for hours.

Then in the dawn, I awoke with clarity. Control, insecurity, fear mongering . . . an unfortunate familiarity with this behavior. Pitting me against peers to keep down mutiny attempts.

While dating the man who became my second husband, I read a magazine article on manipulative relationships. In the middle of the article, on a treadmill at my gym, I got nauseous and ran to the bathroom to throw up. Publicly, I blamed it on a hangover from the night before, but I knew the truth. The article said to get out, as fast as possible, and not to look back. Visions of those written words echoed in my memory for years, and they were all I could think of at that moment.

I should have walked straight away that morning. I had savings; I was employable. But in the words of Maye Musk, "I was determined not to leave until I got what I wanted, and eventually they agreed." Something in me wanted to leave on my terms and to somehow get them to give me everything I wanted. Why sacrifice when I could play the system and simply observe the results?

From that meeting forward, I knew I had a target on my back, and I planned to exploit it for all I could. When a longtime mentor gave me a grave warning—"If you feel as if you have a target on your back, then you likely do"—I knew his words were a thinly veiled warning. When another, more risk averse, mentor told me to get out before they kick you out, it only hardened my resolve.

So, I set out a plan. I would officially follow all the rules while quietly pushing all the buttons and planning my escape. I was in search of a reaction. I was careful to do quality work on behalf of my team. I told them everything and kept them apprised of my plans. I wanted no unintended shrapnel. I distanced myself from colleagues who were equally dissatisfied and regularly back channeling. I got quiet about complaints, nodding with quiet compliance. And I waited for it to all burn down. Disingenuous, perhaps. Revengeful, absolutely. Incongruent with my values, yes.

In the end, I planned exactly how this story would end, and on that day I left quietly, taking a payout to cushion my business relaunch and a release from most of my non-compete. I was finally free. I met a colleague out for a drink and toasted my victory. She shook her head in disbelief. I had gotten exactly what I wanted, and I had done it my way, even when they thought it was theirs. I left with only smoldering embers of the rage I once had. Perhaps so slight as to be undetectable to others. Today I would not trade a single moment. I own every scar. I saw the patterns. I took back the power. I left the cycle.

Doing what is best for you may not always look like the "acceptable" path in other's view. And perhaps that is OK. Sometimes the best way out is through, *if* we are strong enough to take what comes at us, even unexpectedly, and accept the part we played in it.

After leaving this workplace, I relaunched the boutique consulting firm I founded in 2009, InPursuit. Within a year, doors were not just available, they were swinging open with veracity. I worked hard doing top quality work and was rewarded by a continuous string of opportunities. Most importantly I kept my focus on authenticity, humanity, and fun over everything else.

Although I no longer own that binder, its contents were carefully scanned and saved, as was the PowerPoint from that day in in the city.

Every so often, I find those digital files and reflect, not to relive the pain of the days but to relish in the growth that has transpired since.

When the chanting and prayers concluded, I walked out into a night sky dotted with starlight. As I made my way from the monastery to the tea house, I felt a literal 1000 pounds lighter than when I arrived. I could say it was a state of total Zen but the truth is, it was the freedom of knowing exactly what "Fuck around and find out" really feels like. It was the freedom to know I was strong enough to take the punches and still win the fight.

Chapter 8:
Dingboche

Altitude: 4,360m/14,300ft
Travel Time: Five to six hours walk
Soundtrack: Sitting on Wings, DJ Taz Rashid

Ascending along the stone steps, we see the National Park Head Office as we pass by Deboche. Following up the path, we reach Pangboche where a religious place called Pangboche Gompa exists. Walking over some flat trails, passing tea shops, we arrive at Dingboche.

At dawn, I lead a yoga class for the group before embarking on the day's trek to our next destination. Walking east within Imja Tsha valley, the path leads to Chukkung. The air was thin as the altitude gains. At Chukkung, there are few teahouses lending itself to a superb view of the snowcapped peaks and glaciers. We pause here for pictures against the whimsical skyline. As the day progresses, I am relieved at the flexibility I have gained from the morning yoga practice and reflect on the symbolism of other ways yoga has saved me.

Choreographed Chaos

As the water was ran through my fingers, I looked up and caught a glimpse of the flyer taped to the bathroom mirror. A sixteen-day trip to India. Moving my eyes to the reflection in the mirror, I barely recognized the girl who stared back at me. Even the long blonde ponytail and latest lululemon gear could not hide the exhausted and hollow look in her eyes.

I was winding down a relationship with a fun-loving man with a larger-than-life smile and kind eyes. Unfortunately, despite his corporate and personal success, his first love was the bottle followed closely by the grass. After two and a half years, it was clear this was not a path I could continue walking. Untangling lives, regardless of the mutuality, is always messy and painfilled. Perhaps this trip was exactly what I needed to turn the page.

Three months later, I stroll through the automatic door and am hit with a blast of cold air-conditioning meant to counter the humid Florida weather. Even in November, it's impossible to escape the heat. While I usually recoil from the overabundance of AC, today I appreciate it, as I know where we are headed there will be no such thing for many days.

Arriving at the gate, I see the only familiar face: my friend Roni, the owner of the yoga studio and our host. I settle into the hard blue chairs and scroll mindlessly through my phone, when I hear the woman next to me say her own name in third person. A pretty brunette, slightly shorter than me with a spunky energy I instantly adored. As she hung up, I introduced myself as her roommate for the trip, admitting my eavesdropping. And just like that…we were bonded.

India can only be described as frenetic, in the best possible definition. It is a country with an energy of constant motion and our trip was planned to mimic that energy. I waffled between nausea and exhilaration as we took our inaugural rickshaw, or "tuk tuk," ride through town. The streets were a dance of choreographed chaos. Winding our way between bikes, cars, carts, and cows, our senses were overwhelmed. Waves of both delicious and revolting smells wafted through the air as the noise of car horns, cart bells, and yelling became deafening.

Crossing streets amidst the chaos is akin to a life-size 1980s game of Frogger. Needing cash for an upcoming excursion, I followed our trip guide off the bus and waited for his cue to run through traffic. Suddenly, in seemingly slow motion, a small taxi runs head on into an older man on a bicycle. The crunch of his head smacking the pavement is a sound I will never forget.

I let out a loud gasp and ran back onto the bus. Noticing my sheet white glazed expression, my tripmates inquired what I had just witnessed. I began fumbling to find words when the guide steps back on the bus. With a tone of complete confusion he says, "Do you not still need money?"

"I do but...but...," I stammered. "Doesn't he need an ambulance? Shouldn't we help him?"

Now understanding my reaction, he begins to chuckle. "He's fine, just look."

To my amazement, the man was slowly walking his mangled bike past our bus window. His head bloody but less than anticipated. Turning his tone from laughter to wisdom, he tells us, "He was riding the wrong way. He knows better. Perhaps he is drunk."

And just like that, the mystery of the chaos unveiled a powerful lesson. There are cultural norms in every facet of the human experience. Our lack of understanding does not prevent them from being true. What I saw as a tragic accident needing immediate attention was seen in Delhi as the appropriate consequence for ignoring known societal expectations. A consequence he is expected to take full responsibility for. How different from the constant coddling and blame games we play in America. How different indeed.

We arrive at our very first destination, an ancient temple that had been overtaken by Muslim invaders centuries earlier and promptly defaced to remove all the intricate carvings of people dancing and playing music. Despite it being an open-air venue, it was still a working mosque, so in order to enter we were required to done robes. Resembling circus attire more than religious pageantry, the bright blue, green, and red robes with white polka dots made our group stand out even more than our mostly young, mostly women, mostly blonde American traits. We spent an hour walking silently among the pillars and admiring the intricate architecture. I was aware people were staring and a few were following us, but only as we gathered to take a group photo, did I realize the enormity. Turning to face our guide, we realized he was not the only photographer. A group of twenty to thirty strangers all had cell phones out to capture our group as if celebrity status. Noting the hilarity of the moment, we each took our phones out to capture them reciprocally.

Over the next sixteen days, we would experience a full myriad of life. Upon each arrival, we were welcomed with leis of flowers. At dawn each morning, we would come together for yoga. The grass in back of the hotel in Bundi would prove soft and welcoming despite the humid damp air. The covered amphitheater stage made of pure white marble in Udaipur would leave bruises on my knees and elbows from cow pose and funky crow.

We rode camels along the shoreline in Udaipur before taking boats to an island created as a King's private getaway. We donned henna tattoos and headscarves as we entered Buddhist Temples, Hindu Mandirs, and Muslim shrines in Bundi and Ajmer. Outside of Delhi, we sat cross-legged with school children in pressed catholic style uniforms as they excitedly asked us about American culture.

Outside of Jaipur, we stayed one night in an authentic ashram. We gleaned knowledge from the resident guru while carrying out the expected chores of cleaning and food preparation. We sat in long meditations and engaged in lively closed-eyed dancing. All of it awkward and uncomfortable. All of it unequivocally freeing.

And in Agra, we met the Taj. In all my travels, no physical structure has ever left such a lasting impression as the Taj Mahal. As my travel companions and I walked through the gates, a strange calm came over the group and my eyes involuntarily welled. It was simply breathtaking.

The Nobel Prize-winning poet Rabindranath Tagore called the Taj Mahal a "teardrop on the cheek of time" and First Lady Eleanor Roosevelt felt that its white marble "symbolizes the purity of real love." The Taj was built by the fifth Muslim ruler of India as a memorial for his third wife, Mumtaz Mahal. This was a woman he loved and trusted so deeply that he empowered her to make kingdom decisions during his rule. A concept so unheard of in the Muslim tradition and at that time in history, that it ignited speculation and contempt by many. She was known for her work with the poor and for the economic vitality of the kingdom. When she died after childbirth, the emperor's inconsolable mourning went on for decades.

The Taj took twenty-two years to complete and employed 20,000 people to hand carve each individual marble and semi-precious stone piece. Although skeptics have come forth attempting to debunk the romantic nature of this structure, the hand crafted semi-precious stones that lay within each section including only the deceased empress's favorite flower designs tell a different story. It was an economic driver in the kingdom like none had been prior. But more, it was a labor of love— true love and true loss. The gesture was grand and standing in its presence today you cannot help but feel its intensity.

I am not completely convinced modern love is any more or less complicated than the tradition laden days of old but despite the centuries, we are perhaps no more skilled at handling it either. So many of us toggle between our own self-preservation causing us to hold ourselves away from experiencing the deepest part of love. Or conversely so in need of partnership that we sacrifice authentic love for companionship. With the inundation of social media and societal conceptions, do we even know what love really is anymore?

On the final night, we received a priceless invitation to participate in a private Diwali celebration in the home of a family. For nearly the first time in weeks, we carefully prepared our clothing and makeup for the special evening. The anticipatory energy was electric as we gathered in the hotel lobby to await our transport bus. As it arrived, our group sent up a cheer so animated the entire hotel staff turned to stare. Our guides had decorated the bus interior with lights, flowers, and streamers to mark the occasion. It was gorgeous. We boarded and began our journey an hour or so outside of town.

Along the ride the mood was pure party. Despite our complete sobriety, we played music, danced in the bus aisles, and waved at passing cars, bikes, and pedestrians. Can you imagine how entertaining, i.e., silly, this group of Americans must have looked to Indian passersby?

The laughter was boisterous and the time flew by. Soon we were departing the bus and making our way down a long narrow street. The houses on each side were nearly identical to one another—rectangular, tall, and narrow with a flat rooftop. Most were decorated with twinkling, colored lights, candles, and elaborate colored rice designs representative of Diwali.

Our designated home was midway down the street on the right-hand side, hard to miss as the light display seemed larger than any other covering every inch of the wrought iron gate and home entry way. We knew from our guides this invitation was rare and our hosts had gone to extreme measures to prepare for us. We removed our shoes at the door and made our way into the small living room.

The scent of marigolds and flickering candlelight greeted us, as the Pujari, or Hindu Priest, adorned our foreheads with the traditional Sindoor red dot. A small altar sat on the floor glistening with intricate gold carvings, sacred statues, and small offering bowls of flower petals, spices, and fruit.

We took our place on the blankets covering the cold tile floor, and our heads were covered with beautifully woven scarves of red. As the Pujari performed the ceremony, our hosts whispered explanations to us in English as best they could without disruption.

Like so many times in life when I found myself in unfamiliar territory, I ceased trying to understand on an intellectual level and simply absorbed the moment. The sounds of the prayers and chanting, the shadows cast on the wall from the candles, the heat of the room, the smells of the spices. It was a rare moment of complete emersion. A few days earlier, we rode elephants up a small dusty trail in Jaipur to a former castle on a hill. The experience had brought my new friend and roommate, Lana, to uncontrollable tears. In this room, I had my equivalent moment. Holding back the actual tears, I shared in the emotional overwhelm; by the energy, the scenery, the beauty. And perhaps equally by what it represented for my life.

This trip was yet another turning of a page in the book of life. Exploring a country and culture completely foreign while simultaneously exploring the parts of my own soul similarly foreign.

Once the ceremony concluded, we were escorted up a small metal staircase to the home's rooftop. Tables were fashioned with white tablecloths overlain with purple satin, the chairs in shiny gold. A long and luxurious buffet was set on the far side and the smell of gulab jamun, kalakand, shahi tukda, and vegetable samosas wafted through the air.

From that vantage you could see similar, albeit less ornate, versions of this scene across the neighborhood. In the far distance you could see the lights of Delhi twinkling like a faraway galaxy.

Full plate in hand, I found a table and was nearly instantly lost in conversation with a woman in a royal blue sari a few years my junior. She had recently graduated from the University of North Carolina Medical School and returned to India to work for a medical organization serving in the slums on the southeast side of Delhi. Curiously, I tiptoed into a question I could not help but ask. In sixteen days, we had witnessed the heights of wealth in Udaipur, the most sacred historical landmarks in Agra, and the depths of poverty outside Ajmer. What draws her to work with those in such dire circumstances? After all, with her class status and American medical education she could command a lucrative career nearly anywhere in the world.

She paused for a moment as her big brown eyes went hazy with deep introspection. Turning back to me, she simply said, "I guess it's love."

Before another word could be spoken the skies lit up with the boisterous bang of fireworks. As if on a universal cue, rooftops as far as the eye could see began shooting off enormous colored lightshows. They were incredibly close by cautious American standards, only adding to the magic of the moment.

As the colors flashed through the heavens, a familiar sound filled the air. The host's teenage son had equipped his laptop with American pop music, now playing louder and louder from the far corner of the roof. His gift to us, his parents would later inform us. As the group made our way toward the music, the young boy transformed into a great showman, dancing, singing, and daring us to join in.

I was never able to inquire further with the young doctor about her definition of love. But intrinsically, I knew. Love of the vulnerable, love of the downtrodden, love of humanity, love in the form of service.

Making Space

In 2006, I timidly walked through the glass door to a strip mall, one-room yoga studio. Sixteen years later, it is a decision that continues to define my life. Yoga is my safe place, my joy, and the only medicine to truly heal me.

But all I knew on that day was I had to do something for me. I was knee deep in the toxicity that was my personal life, running and lifting weights every day, drinking every night, and working crazy hours in a feeble attempt to drown out the rest. I needed a place to be still, a skill I have always been particularly terrible at.

In a single class, I was sold. Not only did the stillness settle my swirling mind, it also connected with a deeper part of my soul. It was the tiny string that reconnected the dots between who I once was and who I had become.

I took my first dance lesson at four years old. While not the prima ballerina, I was, in fact, naturally talented. When I was out of my head and in my body, I could connect with breath and movement and music in a way that felt nearly spiritual. For the next fifteen years dance became the center of my universe. First classical ballet and tap, then modern and jazz and, when old enough, pointe. Eventually, I merged my dance and singing talents into musical theatre and miscellaneous talent competitions. Body, movement, breath, music was the connective tissue of my childhood.

After making a conscious choice to attend a large university over a performing arts college, I fed that flame through my job as a Disney character and dancer and on campus talent opportunities like Miss UCF pageants and Panhellenic musical competition shows.

Arriving in Miami for graduate school was a system shock on all fronts. I had followed my college boyfriend to the university, but we were desperately poor in a city of flashy wealth. I had no money for dance lessons, no outlet for singing, and no connections for jobs in any entertainment I was willing to do. In this creative wasteland, all of my talent slowly began to die, leaving behind a cavern of longing to reconnect with my body and my voice.

> *Shamans will often ask someone who is depressed, "When did you forget to sing? When did you forget to dance? When did you stop finding refuge in silence? When did you stop being enchanted by stories?"*

> Rebes Bennett,
> *Oh, God!* Podcast

And then, on that chilly February evening, I sat on a mat for the first time and it all began to come together. I began to ask these questions of my soul. Questions I was longing to not only ask but to answer.

Yoga quickly began to feel like coming home. Home to my body with its grace and flexibility, lasting even now in my mid-forties. Home in my breath where I can create heat or calm on my whim. Home in my soul, where the pain of life's disappointments can build until I allow it to release.

In 2019, I took my place among many others as a certified instructor. Never really intending to teach, I simply longed for the depth of knowledge that comes with deeper study. The type of financial splurge that perfectly fit my education values. Over nine months the training taught me the history of yoga, reminded me of the fundamentals of anatomy, and enhanced my empathy for those with body insecurities.

When I left my toxic corporate job, I was wrecked with emotional and intellectual battle scars. There was work to be done on my soul. So once again, I began by simply showing up. Twice a week, I walked through those doors, made space on my mat, and left the world behind.

My muscles were stiff and my poses rusty, but it made no difference. I was there, doing the work, healing my soul.

Not long into this process, I began to see a recurring vision during savasana. A metal pipe, approximately two inches in diameter. It was filled with a yellow-brown gunk that was clogging its ability for the water to flow. Each class I attended, the vision would start to be chipped away. Small pieces, then large chunks, it was clearing. A literal illustration of the healing my own soul was doing, one class at a time.

In *The Body Keeps the Score*, Dr. Bessel van der Kolk elaborates on a common concept. The body is a physiological recording device, capable of documenting every trauma and holding it. In yoga, we commonly say we must release the *issues in our tissues*. But there is science behind that colloquialism. Healing from trauma must be done not only at the intellectual and emotional level but also in the physical body. And it cannot be forced out, through an act of control. Quite the opposite. It must be released by letting go of control and welcoming the empty space that emerges. Empty space that can feel foreign and frightening. Space that our instinct is to fill immediately with something we can control. But healing comes from that uncomfortable space. Healing rolls in like a quiet wave kissing a lake shore. Healing is acceptance and release.

A friend once complained to me that despite upping her yoga attendance to multiple times per week, she was still finding her body stiff and inflexible. Upon inquiry, I learned she was treating yoga with the same forced ferocity she treated every activity in her life. Attending only the hardest power classes, pushing herself to master poses, clenching her metaphorical fists around the idea of yoga's benefits. There was no room for space, no capacity for release. The ambitious characteristics that treated her so well in other parts of life were the exact blocks keeping her from fully embracing the depths of yoga's power.

146

Yoga, at its core, is breath or prana. Prana is the most basic principle of yoga. It roughly translates to life force, vital air. It literally stands for the connection we have between our soul and our breath. It is a subtle energy, which invigorates and enlivens all living beings. This is the literal and metaphorical reason yoga is healing. When we live through trauma, wallow in regrets, or carry unnecessary burdens, we often begin to hold our breath.

Since that fateful day in 2006, each and every time life has come at me with pain I have countered with breath. At times it took far too long to realize I was holding my breath, but eventually I made my way back to the mat and I exhaled.

We arrived into Dingboche around 4:00 p.m. and settled into the main tea hut for our ritualistic ginger tea and rustic naan bread snack. We would spend two nights here to help acclimate to the altitude before continuing our journey.

The next morning, we arose at dawn to hike to Nangkar Peak (5,083m/16,676ft). While the air was crisp, it was warm enough in the bright sunshine to wear shorts for the day. It took approximately three hours to reach the top but once there, the view was remarkable. We were rewarded with the awe-inspiring views of the three highest peaks in the world above 8,000m: Mt. Lhotse (8,749m), Mt. Makalu (8,463m), Mt. Cho Oyu (8,201m), and other mountains such as Island Peak, Ama Dablam, Taboche, Kangtega, and Cholatse. We could also see Imja Valley and Imja Glacier.

The group dispersed to take in views and take photos from various angles around the peak. The girls and I decided to try our hand at yoga on the rocks. I made my way to the highest point I could find with a flat segment of rock to use as a base. And then I began. Standing in a basic mountain pose, or Tadasana, I closed my eyes and just breathed. In…out…in…out.

As my mind wandered, a realization crept over me. In mountaineering, the death zone refers to altitudes above a certain point where the pressure of oxygen is insufficient to sustain human life for an extended time span. This point is generally considered to be anything above 8,000 meters, a distance only 2,700 meters higher than I was perched. And yet, here I was, breathing in and out freely, rotating through a classic yoga sequence of Surya Namaskar or Sun Salutation A. How fickle is the reality of life? How fleeting. The words to describe such a moment are beyond any capacity I hold. I can only lean on others.

> *Every man's life ends the same way. It is only the details of how he lived and how he died that distinguish one man from another.*
>
> Ernest Hemingway

Will the details of my own life distinguish my legacy? Can I leave an imprint on the world, without being a mom? Like the young doctor from a country faraway, can I find a way to transform my talents into love? On this day, standing on a narrow flat rock in Virabhadrasana, nearly above the clouds, this was the prayer I breathed into the universe. May I leave even just one person better for my presence. And it remains my prayer every day since.

Chapter 9:
Lobuche

Altitude: 4,939m/16,207ft
Travel Time: Five to six hour walk
Soundtrack: It Was a Sin, The Revivalists

B eginning from Dingboche, we head towards Lobuche walking
over the mani stones. Taking gradual steps, we will follow the
trail of Three High Passes Trek. The trek is quite strenuous as
we need to cross Kongma La Pass that resides at an altitude of 5,535m.
Moving forward, we pass by the High Camp, a sacred place to honor
those killed on the mountain.

The multicolor Nepalese prayer flags flap in the wind as we sit in
silence. Some wander off to various corners to pray or meditate. Some
wander through the various rock statues. I find a large rock with a view
of the vista and settle in. Inevitably tears well up in my eyes. The energy
is palpable and overwhelming. What is this energy that will bring on such
a rush of emotion? Is it a blessing or a curse to be so intensely aware of
swirling energy and so deeply moved?

Blue Butterflies

"Just concentrate on the blue butterfly." My mother's words echo in my mind each time I stepped onstage to sing.

Our church had a large circular stained-glass window with four distinct quadrants. The only one I recall was the top left which held a large blue butterfly. It would sparkle in the morning sunlight, and I could project the fluttering of my nervous energy onto the fluttering of those sparkling wings.

Although no *American Idol* star, in this small-town church, I held my place as a regular soloist. Sunday morning hymns, valentine fundraisers, holiday and summer musical extravaganzas, and Sunday night youth bonding over acoustic guitars. Music was the lens through which I could understand the world. And in that little church, it is the lens through which I could understand God.

My connection to spirituality runs deep. It's the core of how I choose to live my life. But it doesn't look like any single traditional religious teaching. I haven't stepped inside a church outside of a holiday in nearly two decades. I am viscerally opposed to the trappings of pageantry associated with services and the hypocrisy that rages when religion is used to push political agendas.

I grew up in a progressive, loving, and highly welcoming church, sheltered from the negative aspects of religion, spared of harsh judgement and hypocrisy. It was a place I felt love, acceptance, and encouragement. It was also a place of relevance and inspiration.

Dr. Herb Sadler was a scholar of great literature as well as a religious devotee. His sermons would perfectly interlace classic themes of great modern writers with biblical lessons and then seamlessly overlay them into the news and world events of the day. Perhaps the only man I have ever known who could intuitively know what weighed heavy on his parishioners' hearts and offer them both a biblical lens as well as inspiration from other great historians and documentarians of the world. Through these illustrations, I grew to interpret both God and my own soul.

It was not until I left for college that the bubble of religious graciousness was abruptly burst. As a freshman in college, I found a small but modern church on the edge of campus and began to attend Sunday services. The look of the sanctuary and the feel of the pews was the same, but it held none of the loving energy I was accustomed to. As the weeks drew on, I felt more and more disillusioned. In this minister, I heard no words of modern literary wisdom or acknowledgement of the state of the world. In fact, there was little connection to the modern world at all. What good are these learnings if I cannot parlay them into my everyday life? The disenchantment grew only stronger as I arrived week after week, alone, nearly ghostlike in my anonymity. There were no friendly faces to welcome me, no friends to be made. It was just me in a nondescript pew, halfway back in the sanctuary, singing hymns and desperately grasping for spiritual connection that lit my heart on fire.

As I traveled the world, I studied and appreciated the best and worst of religious traditions. Religion can be beautiful as a source of strength, healing, and connection. But it can also be incredibly ugly. People are shamed, wars are waged, lives are ruined, all in the name of religion. And it enrages me.

If what we know about Jesus is true, he was undoubtably the prophet who taught us more about love than perhaps any other human being in history. He consistently ignored or even denied exclusionary or punitive texts in his own Jewish Bible in favor of passages that emphasized inclusion, mercy, and honesty. As he traversed a tumultuous world, he stopped to really see people and make them feel valued for who they were. He loved the unwanted as fiercely as he loved the prominent. Perhaps this is why I am so deeply offended by the bastardization of that love by those who spew only hate in the name of so-called Christian faith. In particular, the wave of politicians who have taken up discrimination and the restriction of human rights based on completely false doctrine.

Over my life, I have become more resolute about my own version of spirituality. I believe the best way to honor my Christian upbringing is to love people for who they are, not stereotypes we hold of people "like them." I believe it is everyone's right to hold themselves to whatever values and standards they wish, but it is not our right to force those standards on others. While you may consider abortion or homosexuality a sin, I see no justification for judgement of others for their beliefs or choices. Who are you to throw stones? In fact, the more shade people throw at others, the more ferociously I want to stand and defend them.

> *Spirituality is not to encourage willfulness, but in fact willingness. Spirituality creates willing people who let go of their need to be first, to be right, to be saved, to be superior, and to define themselves as better than other people.*
>
> Dr. Gerald May

As a deeply intuitive human, I can instantaneously sense a person's humanity. And to me this is the absolute most important aspect of human connection. I do not care who you love, what color your skin is, who you worship, what you do for a living, or what mistakes you might have made in your life. I simply cannot comprehend why any of that matters in the slightest.

In contrast, I am fiercely in love with the best in the human spirit. With the depths of our heart and our intentions. I care whether or not you have empathy for your fellow human. I care whether or not you make daily decisions based in kindness, love, and acceptance. I care about selflessness and humility in a world where narcissism and greed are prominent.

All religious texts, including the Bible, were written by humans, specifically men, and are therefore inherently biased.

> *The Bible is actually a conflict book. It is filled with seeming contradictions or paradoxes, and, if you read it honestly and humbly, it should actually cause problems for you. The way you struggle with the fragmentation of the Bible is the way you probably struggle with your own fragmentation and the fragmentation of everything else. The Bible offers you a mirror that reflects back to you how you live life in general.*

> Richard Rohr

In this purview, I look to my own heart and intuition for spiritual guidance. I must trust in my personal connection to God and my unique lens on the world to lead my actions.

While we are all imperfect, intent matters. I am viscerally sickened by discrimination, whether overt or subtle. Built in fear and a need for power—from Putin and Russian invasion to US laws against LGBTQIA+ and book burning—they are led by those with deep insecurities about their own worth.

Everything exposed to the light itself becomes light.

Ephesians 5:13

We don't need to exert dominance when we are confident and grateful. I often fantasize about being locked in a room with those with the greatest hate in their heart and just continuously asking them what are they so afraid of? What inadequacies are they making up for with all this need for persecution? Why wouldn't we want to expose our own weaknesses—as a country, as a society, as a human—in order to transform it to something better? If we are truly the highest version of humanity, we need only to wake up and love others including what we perceive as their "flaws" and allow God to do the rest. Jesus taught love over hate, and yet all the repressive legislation and hate speak in the name of Christianity seems to have forgotten that.

> *The egocentric will still dominate: the need to be right, the need to be first, the need to think I am saved and other people are not. This is the lowest level of human consciousness and God cannot be heard from that heady place or be met at that level.*

Richard Rohr

Calling Uncle

After less than a year, I left that little church outside campus and never went back. Anywhere. For the next decade, my presence in a church was an occasional obligatory holiday with the family or a friend's wedding. During this time, I searched and found meaning in the study of other religious traditions, in meditation and yoga, and in the very rare silent prayers to a God who felt a million miles away. But something in my soul ached for more.

And then one day, in my late-thirties under a cloud of depression, I sat on the floor and called uncle on the silent treatment I was giving God. And I was welcomed back with open arms. In the months that followed, in my own way with my own parameters, we embarked on a relationship again. Far from perfect, my goal each morning became honoring that blue butterfly, my own visual representation of God, by loving others through my time, talents, and treasures. And my goal each night is to give grace for my imperfections and gratitude for the chance to be alive.

Abraham-Hicks says, "A belief is just a thought you keep thinking." In creating my own version of spirituality, I took time to define my own beliefs, intellectually, and intuitively. And then I leaned on those beliefs in times of joy and times of sorrow.

To this day, you will rarely hear me speak of God, making this particular writing a challenge to surmount. I do not believe my strength is the articulation of faith, but rather the embodiment. For me I choose action over words.

Big Brown Eyes

My hands were blistered beneath the heavy leather work gloves, and my contacts were stinging from the sweat dripped suntan lotion running into them. My back ached, and my biceps were shaking. I had been standing in the same spot for nearly five hours, cutting rebar and bending small metal pieces to fasten around it. We were a small but mighty team of eighteen, trading our Thanksgiving turkey and football for eight days in the blazing sun of rural Nicaragua building houses with Habitat for Humanity International.

In this country, there is no heavy machinery or prefabricated materials. Everything must be done by hand. Each morning, we mixed concrete and mortar in small pits we dug in the earth. To my surprise, only one ingredient separates the two when making them from scratch. We kept the mixtures wet by periodically hauling and dumping buckets of water on them. We made an assembly line to move more than one hundred concrete blocks from the delivery pile to the job site thirty yards away. We stamped concrete floors, built block walls, and as illustrated above, cut rebar—lots and lots of rebar. We had only a set of hand wire cutters to cut the eight-foot sections and plyers to bend the small metal pieces around the bundles of three. After ten bundles were assembled, we called to another team to retrieve and deliver them to the house approximately twenty yards away. It was painstakingly slow and yet, it was extraordinary.

By week's end, we were sore, sunburned, exhausted, and transformed. We had used our physical time and treasures to change the life of one family forever. It may have been only one family, but you only had to look into the big brown eyes of a little girl who was to live in that house to know it was worth every ounce of effort. In the eyes of this little girl, who had been sleeping on the floor in a small room with seven family members her entire life, you could see hope. Hope for a better life. Hope for a more comfortable place to learn, to grow, and to thrive. *This* to me is the best I can ever do for humanity. Service is my religion.

Over the years, I have said yes as often as possible to moments like this one. From urban farming in some of the most economically depressed parts of Baltimore to landscape planting in the cheerful view of animals at the Tampa Zoo. From building handicap ramps for the elderly in Jacksonville to building bunk beds in a Refuge house for domestic violence and sex traffic survivors in Atlanta. From childhood literacy efforts around Florida to food distribution in Colorado. When asked, there is no place I will not travel or initiative with which I will not participate. It is both a selfless and selfish simultaneously. It is my way of giving back to humanity and of repenting for the harm I might inadvertently do on any given day.

> *The good you do today may be forgotten tomorrow. Do good anyway.*

Mother Teresa

Some will say none of these actions is not enough, that it is a form of denial to not speak openly or attempt to persuade others to our beliefs. But who am I? No one knows ultimate truth about spirituality. And each of us are far from a perfect specimen of humanity. We know only what we are taught by readings, ritual, upbringing, or intuition. For me, I seek connection with the latter over all three of the former.

We sit at the High Camp for over an hour, feeling the quiet energy of the hopes, promises, and sorrows that accompanied other's visits. It is difficult for me to stay still, physically and metaphorically. But every day I make the attempt. On this day, I close my eyes and go inside. The sound of the wind swirling mirrors the stirs in my own soul. It whistles in my ears and blows my hair onto my face. The chilled air burns my throat when I breathe in deeply. The rock I am perched upon is cold, hard, and awkwardly shaped. I implore myself to continue to sit. To feel it all. To remind myself I will likely never be back in this place again and

I will certainly never again have this moment in time.

Meditation, like prayer, has documented physical and intellectual benefits even beyond its spiritual components. But so often those who pray have turned the act into asking rather than seeking.

> *The word prayer has often been trivialized by making it into a way of getting what we want. But I use prayer as the umbrella word for any interior journeys or practices that allow us to experience faith, hope, and love within ourselves.*

The Naked Now

Few people really partake in the benefits of meditation. And I can fully relate. For some, perhaps they deny the benefits and see it only as hokum. For others, life's chaos—spouses, kids, work, chores—push it too far down the priority list.

But I believe there is even more to the aversion than this. There is a deeper fear that keeps us away. It is illustrated in our natural frenetic tendency to fill gaps in conversation with useless chatter or the squirming we do in our seats when a group speaker allows uncomfortable silence. We are viscerally afraid of the still, of the silence. Belonging expert Crystal Whiteaker calls this the shadow work. It is scary, but it must be done. But exactly what is it about shadow work that scares us?

A study published in *Science*[1] by Timothy Wilson and his co-authors, social psychologists at the University of Virginia in Charlottesville, uncovered a disheartening fact about modern inward thinking.

---

[1] (July 2014, pg. 75-77)

Individuals were placed in sparsely furnished rooms and asked to simply think. Afterward, the team asked the volunteers to rate their experience on a nine-point scale, where the higher the number, the more enjoyable their time was. Nearly half of the participants did not like the experience. To see if a change of scenery would help, the team let participants do the studies in their own homes, but still found similar results. Overall, the subjects said they enjoyed activities like reading and listening to music about twice as much as just thinking.

The researchers then decided to take the experiment a step further. For fifteen minutes, the team left participants alone in a lab room in which they could push a button and shock themselves if they wanted to. The results were startling: 67% of men and 25% of women chose to inflict pain on themselves rather than just sit there quietly and think. It is hard to fathom this level of discomfort with our own company.

To really be still means to sit with our whole selves. It means laying down the crutch of busyness. It means putting aside our sense of self-importance. It means coming out from the shadow of self-sacrifice for family or others. It is just stillness. Sitting naked in your own soul is a dark and scary place for many of us. But there is simply no other way to truly know yourself, deeply, authentically know who you are. And without knowing who you are, you will never really know what you are capable of and never truly find joy.

> *Only when we are brave enough to explore the darkness will we discover the infinite power of our light.*
>
> Brené Brown

We walk the remaining distance to Lobuche in silence; the sun nearly blinding as it cascades off the mountain snow. We never discussed what each of us quietly contemplated on that sunny afternoon. I think some things are best left between you and your God.

Chapter 10:
Everest Base Camp

Altitude: 5,170m/16,961ft; 5,364m/17,594ft; 6,065m /19,900ft
Travel Time: Eight to nine hour walk each way
Soundtrack: Hell of a View, Eric Church

D espite our exhaustion, by this elevation, no one is truly sleeping. To get any sleep, we are all trying personal body contortions that keep us both warm and allow our bodies to take in enough oxygen to rest. Breakfast conversations became an inevitable string of victories or defeats.

On this day, however, there is an extra spring in our step. It is *the* day we have been waiting for. After a lunch stop in Gorakshep, we will continue on to our ultimate destination—Everest Base Camp. Only summit climbers can get permits to sleep at Base Camp, so after pictures are taken and the glory of the moment is captured, we will descend back to Gorakshep for the night.

The air is so electric, the sun so vibrant, the sky so blue, I barely noticed the far below freezing temperatures. Climbing, we follow Everest Base Camp Trek trail and come across Pyramid Lobuche pass at 5,110m and Tsho Lake before reaching Gorakshep.

On most days, the lunch stop is a welcome reprieve from the hard trek. A time to sit, rest, refuel. We linger over soup and snacks and hot tea until our guides insist we move along in order to make our destination by dark. Today, however, we down anything put in front of us with anticipatory veracity and are outside the shelter waiting on the guides to join. A few hours of regular trekking before turning a corner and there they are. Far in the distance, the string of tiny yellow tents that indicate Everest Base Camp.

One Knee Down

Climbers wishing to summit Everest acclimate at each base camp. Nepal's South Base Camp is considered camp one and the most notable as it begins the summit and ends the more common tourist trek. During climbing season, it holds clusters of bright yellow tents hung with National and Company flags alike.

Without a word, the entire team stops to take in the scene. The first sighting of these tents, far in the distance, is like a beacon. This is the destination we have all worked for over the last seven days and dreamed of for years prior.

The final distance is primarily bouldering. In Colorado, I bemoan unexpected bouldering as the spiderman agility it requires, especially with my short arms and legs, leaves me sore for days. But here, I welcome it. I want to feel it, all of it—the scrapped knees, raw hands, loss of breath, deep ache. I want to remind my mind just what my body is capable of and my body how strong my mind is.

Where hours normally felt like days, these felt like mere moments. In the blink of an eye, we were there, passing by Camp and Pumori BC to reach Everest Base Camp.

As we come off the trail, we spot the enormous boulder that serves as the famous spray-painted elevation picture spot. I take a step toward it when Randy unexpectedly grabs my hand. His words muffled by the high winds and layers of clothes, I understand him to say we are headed up to the emergency helipad, another 1000ft up in elevation. I look around at our group for someone in distress. All seems to be fine, but it is too late to ask. He is already making his way there.

At nearly 18,000 feet in altitude, each step is slow and labored. One hundred meters can take up to an hour to complete, making this additional journey feel arduous and unnecessary. Catching up to Randy, I inquire grumpily on what I am missing. He explains our friends, who had not been able to continue the trek past Namche Bazaar, would be flying in briefly to take photos at Base Camp before returning to lower elevation. I found this an expensive luxury out of character for them; yet I trudged on slowly to higher ground, excited to see them again and happy they would do this for themselves.

The orange windsocks are blowing straight out as we reach the helipad. The sky is thick with heavy white clouds. There is a spirited Nepalese conversation happening between our guides, the helipad operator, and someone on the other end of the radio. I find a block of ice sturdy enough to make a seat and snuggle down into my layers.

Along the trek we have been greeted by many native wild animals. From birds and other small creatures at low elevations to yak and sheep at higher levels. However, dogs have been with us throughout. One particular dog—a version of a wild sheepdog—has followed us all the way from Gorakshep. Still with us at the helipad, he snuggles up beside Randy, who is nervously fidgeting a few meters away.

After more than an hour, we get word the helicopter is on the way. They will be able to stay only five minutes as engine cannot be cut at this elevation or it won't find lift to return.

As the helicopter lands, I rush to hug our friends. It has been only six days since I have seen them but somehow it feels like six years. So much has transpired on this trek. So many self-discoveries, so many memories, so many things we have seen and felt and experienced. I want to share all of it and hear of their adventures as well.

But suddenly I am pulled away by Randy's strong grasp. I spin around completely confused to see him down on one knee. I begin stammering the words "what, what, what is happening?"

Peeling off three layers of gloves, he slips a small Tibetan love band on my hand. In the noise of the wind and helicopter, I have no idea what he actually says in that moment but when his lips stop moving, I jubilantly nod yes and everyone cheers.

Sunflowers and Volcanos

"Oh, I thought you'd be taller."

These were the first words Randy spoke as he opened the door to greet me for our first date. In nearly any other scenario, that would have sent me walking back to my car and driving away. But something about the way he was immediately mortified, apologetic and bumbling to recover made me only smile.

We met a week previous on Bumble and spent the days between sharing travel stories and future dreams via phone and Voxer. I shared with him my past—twice divorced, now going on ten years single. My devotion to travel, the places I had explored so far, and the long list ahead. My disdain for Florida despite having lived there my entire life. And my deeply innate need to adventure and stay in perpetual motion.

Randy is a retired Army Ranger, who spent more than 1,200 days in combat spread between Mogadishu, Iraq, and Afghanistan. He now works for a software company that is embedded in the Department of Defense and has been back to the middle east nine more times in that capacity. Also divorced just under ten years, the real love of his life was his stepdaughter. A beautiful girl he raised who only sees him as Dad.

We set out on what can only be described as a comedy of errors first date. Falling out of an oversized Starbucks chair, getting trapped by the parking garage credit card machine, showing up unexpectedly to a death metal show, and mutilating a poor shrimp in his etouffee; these were the scenes that began our love affair. These are the scenes that built the foundation of laughter that is the glue that keeps us together.

But there was more than laughter on that first night. After all the bloopers, we ended the night on the second floor of the Locale Market. Over a charcuterie board and a whiskey, he opened the book of his life that is permanently inked on his skin. As the hours passed, the vulnerability increased. Each of his many tattoos tells a story—what he saw, what he experienced, and what he hopes to honor. Yet unlike many military veterans, his tattoos were more intentional, symbolic, and artistic, rather than overtly military emblematic. Most meaningful was the sleeve dedicated to his best friend, killed nearly in front of him in Afghanistan.

"I wanted the art to be so beautiful and intriguing that people would ask me about it, and I could talk about Mike."

And in that moment, everything changed. The depth of his vulnerability made him instantly fall-in-loveable. Which is exactly what I did for only the second time in my life.

As I drove home over the Howard Franklin Bridge that night, I rolled down the windows and sang until my voice was hoarse. There was something about this man. In the decade since my divorce and the great chase, I had grown exponentially both professionally and personally. I worked my way up the ladder while working through the drinking, and the guilt of poor early life decisions. But somehow, I still felt tarnished. Either by my past mistakes or my future desires. I had given up notions of the white picket fence suburbia life. Now I wanted the world. After all these years, I had resigned myself to believing perhaps that meant I had to do it all alone. And then he walked in. He didn't think any of my dreams were too big or too crazy. He only wanted to be a part of them.

He showed up at my door twelve hours later with a handful of sunflowers and a heart full of promise. By the end of our second date, I was hooked. I had met my match, my adventure loving soul mate. And we were off to the races. We spent our third date in Hawaii where he was on a work assignment. Both working half days and spending the remaining time together, we hiked volcanos, shopped in boutiques and flea markets, ate pineapple ice cream and spam rolls—all overlaid by

166

endless laughter. Laughing like I had not done in years. Deep, free, carelessly ugly belly laughs, which seemed to only multiply as days went on. How could this man who had seen so much, lived so much, be so lighthearted? Although he could be thoughtful when we talked about subjects of depth, he was never grumpy or brooding. Never taking himself or life too seriously.

"No one's shooting at me today," he would say, "so it's a good day." Putting any complaints I might hold in my mind, completely in context.

We planned to run a 1990s theme color run and created ridiculous decorated tank tops with puffy paint stick on foam graphics. Upon arrival, as the sun was setting, we realized how rocky the course looked and opted for walking, hand-in-hand, the full three miles. He shared with me more about the world he had seen—the beauty and the devastatingly ugly.

We talked through our views on God, life, death, and children. Although he raised his stepdaughter from a toddler and they are still very close, his words held a wistfulness about what having his own child would have been like. The learning of the pregnancy, building a crib, snuggling an infant who might just look like him. I lamented a similar feeling of what if.

Our romance whirlwind didn't stop in Hawaii. He had returned for only a day when I offered him an unexpected slot as my date for a friend's wedding. The day of the ceremony I was fully enthralled with the hustle and bustle of pre-wedding bridesmaid duties. But I stole a glance out the second story window to see how he was doing in a crowd of people he had never once met. I smiled to see his tan suit and pink shirt in the perfect shade to compliment my gown. Nice touch. I loved that I only needed to mention not taking a date for him to want to accompany me. I loved that he would pay attention to my dress color and make the effort to buy a new shirt. I loved that he would show up to a South Tampa mansion knowing not one soul and sit patiently waiting till I was free for that first dance with him.

It was all just real, grounded. It was what love is supposed to feel like. Not forced or contrived, not manipulative or ego driven, not a game or a chase. Just two people who are perfectly happy being alone, choosing to be together instead. And it was enchanting.

The Time Until...

The day after the wedding I left on a solo trip to Peru. It was my fortieth birthday, and something was calling me to the mountains. I boarded a plane to my first overnight camping trek through the Andes Mountains to Machu Picchu. This four-night adventure traversed four mountains before culminating in the valley that holds the ancient ruins. As much glamping as camping, we carried only our clothing and personal supplies. Porters handled our tents and group supplies and pampered us along the way with delicious food. Perhaps my favorite moment of each day was rounding the last corner on the day's trek to the smell of fire roasted vegetables and steaming bowls of homemade soup wafting through the air.

My fellow trekkers, ten in total, all hailed from various parts of the UK. Conversations of Brexit, American politics, and pop culture were the norm. However, by journey's end we had delved much deeper. From childhood memories to painful breakups, from future aspirations to past mistakes, the trail became our therapists' couch.

I knew this would be an experiment for Randy and me. Each so ferociously independent, I hoped he would be comfortable with my solo travel, but knew it required a unique mindset. And yet again, he did not disappoint.

After my first two solo days exploring Cusco, where wi-fi is ample, I headed to the Inka trail where all phone signals were promptly lost. As the only solo traveler of the group, I was gifted a single tent, leaving ample time for me to journal, reflect, and lie alone listening. This trail held a silence I had never experienced. The bubbling brook in the distance, the hooting owl, the rustling of the trees—it seemed almost feigned in its realism. One's soul can often identify important moments in time long before our minds can articulate them. These were such moments. An intrinsic connection to the trail and the earth. An intangible sense of peace in the vastness of the view from the mountain peaks. Indelible marks that prove to foreshadow a future life chapter.

My return from Peru was like a homecoming, as if we had been a couple for six years not six weeks. There was not a hint of negativity about my trip. He listened with genuine interest to every detail. There was no suspicion about my fellow travelers, no passive aggressive jealousy of missing out on the adventure. It was just mature, genuine excitement for me and what I experienced. It was almost unfathomable after what I had been through.

We spent the next five months soaking in every moment of each other. Bike rides and run clubs, weekends away and weekends at home on the boat. We met each other's family and became friends with each other's friends. All the while we tried not to think of the looming deadline ahead. Until it inevitably arrived.

There was drizzling rain on that August morning as we drove to the airport. The swishing of the windshield wipers was the only sound as we both struggled for words. He was headed to Afghanistan, a place of inherent familiarity to him, yet completely foreign to me. He was headed to run his company's operations for the entirety of the country. And I would be holding my breath for the next four months.

Timing is Everything

Randy returned home one week after my surgery, and I exhaled. We made it through those four months, and our life officially began. We moved in together, and then headed west to a place that felt instantly like home. We made a pact to live as close to the edge as we could stand and chase life over money. We made a promise to laugh as hard as we love and to never take ourselves or life too seriously.

Randy and I went on to marry—during a global pandemic inside a clock tower with only fifteen friends and family present. The working clock face backdrop of our ceremony was a powerful illustration of us. It was an event as unique as my own quirky soul. I wore my mom's 1972 wedding dress, adding my personality by donning purple boots and a peacock feather hairpin. I walked down the aisle to a Lady Gaga song. Lana, serving as officiant, got nervous, messed up the script, and proceeded to say fuck at least a dozen times, sending everyone present into fits of laughter. Paying homage to my favorite meal, it was a mid-morning brunch, mimosa and Bloody Mary reception. And Randy and I closed the day by dancing, and singing, to our own choreographed *Ballad of Love and Hate*.

In *The Feminine Mystique*, Betty Freidan describes the societal definition of marriage as, "a complete merging of egos and loss of separateness, a giving up of individuality rather than a strengthening of it." But like the independent, childless couples she writes about, Randy and I had no obligatory reason to wed—societal norm or family pursuit—we simply wanted to.

When I think about my legacy and what might be in my obituary, there will be no standard motherhood reverence to mention. Therefore, I think deeply about what will take its place. I do not want my greatest accomplishment to be how long I made a relationship work. I want it to mention how many people's lives I amplified, how many fantastic adventures I went on, how much I loved and nurtured and cared for others. I want to make an impact on the world that far exceeds any one relationship. Randy's ability to support this mantra has been everything for me. He knows my desire to leave a legacy larger than my marriage, and yet also knows it doesn't reduce the importance of our marriage or the love held within.

The absolute best understanding of the unique version of a couple that is Team Cicks is what a typical hiking day looks like. Randy and I both love hiking. But we hardly ever hike together. Sure, we plan the destination, check in we both have the gear, and drive to the mountain together. But as soon as we begin, we are in separate worlds. Randy is a skilled hiker, far quicker and more sure-footed than I am, which has him far ahead on the trail in mere moments. In fact, I have taught myself to memorize the color of his clothing just so I can pick him out when he becomes a small dot on the landscape ahead. I like to listen to music or a book while I hike; Randy prefers his own thoughts and the sound of the trail. So even when we are in proximity we are not talking. Randy likes to trek hard and then stop to rest. I like to trek at a slow but steady pace and hate to stop unless absolutely necessary. But there is one thing we never do alone—summit. No matter how far ahead he might be,

Randy will pause just below the summit and wait as long as necessary for me to join him. Once together, we put down our poles, clasp hands, and walk the final yards together. We always summit together.

Randy and I both love to indulge in documentaries on travel, adventure, and the world. Often, for no particular reason, a scene from one of these will bring me to tears. In a sentiment I will explore in the next chapter, I often have no idea why. I am simply overcome with emotion. In this scenario, the emotion is part longing, part calling. I long for the way that adventure lights up my soul. I long for the pain that pushing my body—intellectually, emotionally, physically—feels like. And I long to find more ways to explore what I know is my calling. And Randy watches this transpire. Often with the playful exasperation, "Are you crying right now?"

Recently, at a no-frills brewery dinner, on a random Sunday afternoon, he looks over at me and says, "If we sold this house and downsized, you could take your half to have a huge chunk of money to explore the world. I think you should find a way to make that happen."

I stared at him dumbfounded. UH WHAT?!? But what about our marriage, our life, our dogs, my business? He reminds me of the tears that spring up when I see scenes from faraway lands. He reminds me of the way my eyes light up when I have an opportunity to join humanitarian work. He reminds me that he was once a soldier that left his family for twelve to eighteen months at a time and somehow made it work.

"I can't be the person that holds you back from who you are supposed to be."

There is no greater love than this. Full Fucking Stop.

Like all couples, we have our own versions of strife. Days when we bicker or take each other for granted. Times when life moves so fast, we are like ships passing in the night within our own home. But then there are the moments that take away my breath: a dinner party where he gushes about my accomplishments with such pride it makes me blush; dancing around our living room with our dogs, laughing until our sides hurt; a casual story from his military life revealing absolute bravery; his golden heart so full of love for the entirety of humanity without prejudice or judgment. He indulges my love of costume parties and cocktail dresses. He often thinks my big audacious dreams are crazy, but he supports them anyway without the shadow of selfish fear. He is courageous yet humble, deep yet light-hearted. And when he looks at me, I see only love.

This is our life. It moves a million miles an hour. It looks completely different from the one I once envisioned. It looks completely different than others' lives. It's imperfect. But it's our imperfect.

They say that timing is everything. And for Randy and me, that could not be more accurate. Two failed marriages and dozens of misaligned relationships later, there he was. A Bumble match, a comical first date, a bike ride to brunch, and the rest is history. Any other time in life and neither of us would have been ready. I might have run from his unexpected proposal like I had done once before. Or I might have been still longing for the chase.

Everyone's love stories happen in their own way. For Randy and me, both divorced ten years, both fiercely independent, both bearing our unique version of life's battle scars, the timing was perfect. And standing on that glacier at the base of the most famous mountain in the world, it was, indeed, a hell of a view.

Chapter 11:
Pheriche

Altitude: 4,280m/14,070ft
Travel Time: Eight to nine hour walk
Soundtrack: Broken, Lifehouse

We wake early to enjoy the last breathtaking morning view this close as the sun glistens over the snowcapped Mount Everest, Lhotse, and Nupse, and then begin to descend towards Dingboche via Lobuche and finally rest in Pheriche.

By this point in the journey, Randy is very ill and his ability to power through is waning. For the first time, I am deeply concerned about his ability to make the rest of the trek. In Pheriche, we find a Doctors Without Borders clinic where a chatty English doctor assures us that an antibiotic and the descent to lower elevation will heal his debilitating cough within a few days, which is a relief for now. A sense of gratitude and relief washes over me, coupled with extreme sleep deprivation, and I begin to unintentionally and uncontrollably cry, and then laugh at the ridiculousness.

Crying Eyes

I have always been quick to cry. Whether or not I want to, a surge of hot tears accompanies nearly every intense emotional response I exhibit. Like most, I release sadness through tears—from losing loved ones to heartaches to failures. But the list is much longer than those expected moments. I cry at commercials, songs, and random acts of kindness I witness on the street. I cry at sunrises, moments in nature, and high-rise views that take my breath away. I cry at powerful speeches or historical moments. I have even been known, much to Randy's dismay, to begin crying out of nowhere over a series of thoughts only in my mind with seemingly no trigger.

For years, I tried to hide this tendency to the best of my ability, ashamed of the attached perception of weakness it occupies. I have been teased by peers who find humor in it, caused panic in past lovers based on their own fears of emotional vulnerability, and chastised by a patriarchal workplace pretending strength lies only in being hardened to humanity.

However, crying for me is a cathartic experience. A release of emotion that cannot be replaced in any other manner. Whether simply misty-eyes, one hot tear rolling down my cheek, or full-on ugly alligator sobbing, I now choose to accept this as part of myself as one more sign of beauty within my full self and a physical representation of the deep level of empathy I hold for others.

A Dentist's Prayer

Sometimes the burdens we carry become uncovered at the most unexpected times—like a dentist chair on a random Tuesday. It is in those moments we experience either the best or worst of humanity. On this day, I was blessed with an angel in the form of a dental hygienist who was not only patient with my alligator tears but took her own empathy to the next level.

The office was icy cold despite the bustling of patients and staff. Having recently moved to the city, I was a new patient in the office. As I sat in the chair enduring the required x-rays and preliminary examination requirements.

3...4...4...5...4...5....

The hygienist began calling out my gum measurements. Healthy gums should show one to three millimeters, a fact I prided myself on maintaining. But those were not my numbers today. I stopped her counting and inquired, just to be sure I was not misremembering. She confirmed my gums seemed inflamed and receding. Something was wrong.

I am fortunate to hold a history of healthy teeth sparing me any true dental office nightmares. Despite this fact, today I was overly tense and squirming against the hard cushions of the chair. The toxic environment of my work left me living on a perpetual short fuse. Feeling crushed daily by the overwhelming cultural negativity while balancing unhealthy workloads and the extreme narcissism of our company's leader. Could this be manifesting in my body? My teeth?

And then, without warning, I began to cry. Not just cry but all out sob. It was simply a last straw. I could no longer rationalize away the stress that was wrecking my emotions, my mental health, and now my physical health.

Looking up, I saw the hygienist's face soften from her initial shock into a calm and resolute smile. I needn't say anything to explain. She seemed to just know.

"May I pray for you?" she asked.

While my visceral reaction to overtly religious acts is withdrawal, in that moment all I could do was nod. She laid her hands softly on my arm and simply asked for God to bless me. To remove the burdens weighing heavily on my soul. When she finished, she quietly went back to measuring and cleaning my teeth. Not a word more was said about it. My tears dried, and I slipped out of the office as if in a dream. I never saw her again, but her impact is forever seared in my psyche.

Empathy can appear in many varieties, the deepest of which requires no words of explanation, and no closure. It is just given, when and where it is needed, in the best ways we know how. At times we are drawn to show our empathy for those right in front of us. While other times, we can only quietly let it out to the universe for the burdens others were forced to bear.

Cellar Dashes

I hung up the phone and laughed out loud. An acquaintance that would later become a best friend had just bought her ticket to join me in Europe. Her disbelief in my plans to travel alone compelled her to surprise me for the accompanying adventure. And what an adventure it was to be.

After a night to ourselves toasting champagne in London, we joined the group of Australians who would be our companions for the following six countries and ten days.

We ate decadent waffles dipped in gooey Nutella in Belgium. We danced alongside ten-foot-tall robots in the foggy haze of a Berlin club. We marveled at the art along the former Berlin Wall. We walked solemnly through a memorial and museum dedicated solely to the news and media during the Holocaust tragedy. We sat inside a still unrepaired French church bombed during WWII. We cruised along the Amstel River gazing at the row houses in the former red-light district. We laughed our way through an abhorrent Prague puppet show and a train misdirection leaving us with armloads of shopping bags on a platform flanked by two pit bulls on large chains in the Czech Republic. We bought endless Ampelmann trinkets and hangover snacks while *I Love it* by Icona Pop and Charlie XCX played endlessly on repeat. Each of these memories is sacred to me. And yet, there is one that will echo in my mind for a lifetime.

The thunder clapped loudly as we stood in the lobby of our hotel. Our plans for the evening to join a large street watch party for the futbol match washed away with the rain. The group split for a free night in its stead. Approximately eight of us dodged the rain and headed to a Mexican restaurant a few blocks up a cobblestone side street. Hours filled with margaritas, tequila shots, and strange European versions of tacos passed in seemingly seconds. As the servers began sweeping the floor a man approached our table. Medium height and slight build, he was intrigued by our raucous group. Explaining our international tourist makeup, he introduced himself as the owner and pulled a chair to join us.

Before long he was regaling us with the history of his family as well as the building. This restaurant space had been in his family for decades. Once traditional German food, his father had converted it to Mexican after a trip to Tijuana many years prior. However, culinary history was only the beginning. He implored us to walk outside with him. Looking up to the roofline, we stood mesmerized as the rain drizzled down our faces. The building had been bombed during the war and the highly decorative original exterior had a definitive diagonal scar where new repair had been added with strict austerity rather than matching beauty.

Even before we knew the term Instagram-worthy, American culture prioritized synchronicity and aesthetics above all. We are quick to tear down, to build new, to cover the old, the ugly, the historic with the décor craze of the moment. It would be unimaginable for a building in our country to maintain this visible scar that represents such national shame. Ironically, it is more likely we deny our past sins than to allow the simple truths to remain visible.

As we file back inside, he offers us the chance to see one more secret treasure of the old building. The wooden planks creek as he moves away a heavy storage cart to expose a cellar door. Taking a key from his pocket he removes the bolt lock and tugs the door ajar. One finger in the air, he descends into the darkness before a moment later popping up his head and waving his flashlight for us to follow.

The cellar was cold and the smell of damp dirt permeated throughout. We followed past a small maze of wooden crates with familiar vegetable names stamped on the side in German. And then without warning, he stopped and shined his flashlight down a hallway of stalls. He explained these were built nearly 100 years earlier as winter holding pens for animals and later used as overstock storage. He cautioned us to duck as we moved to stand inside one of the pens. His flashlight lingered on a crossbeam about four feet off the ground. Carved in the side was an inscription I could not read next to seemingly endless dashes.

Imploring us with unnecessary but ingrained secrecy, the restaurant owner parlayed the full story of the pens. During the Holocaust, his family took in refugee Jews from the nearby neighborhoods. Most were regular customers or vendors of their restaurant, others were strangers. He said over the years of the war up to thirty families occupied the cramped space, each claiming one pen as their "home." Using the bustle and noise of the restaurant as cover, they were able to converse, study lessons, and pray during business hours. They also had regular supply of food and water thanks to the owners.

The restaurant had been ransacked by Nazi Gestapo twice during those years and each time they were able to evade persecution by twist of fate. The first, a random investigation by an overly ambitious but young squad missed the cellar door altogether. After demanding a bribe of the full night's earnings, they left without incident. The second, brought on by a tip from a nervous employee, fled the cellar at the sound of incoming air fire mere steps away from the back pen where three families were crouching together.

We stood for a long moment in silence, and I was struck by the stark contrast of the frivolity of our gathering on the floor above and the historical heaviness of this unknown world just below us.

You could hear the proverbial pin drop as we trudge the wet streets back to the hotel. As I lay in bed that night, the magnitude of what I witnessed overwhelmed me and I began, of course, to cry.

While writing this work Russia's unprovoked invasion of Ukraine left the world to watch in horror and disgust as one man's insecurities, fear, and greed led to the displacement of millions and the deaths of thousands.

For Randy and me, the news was all-consuming. His military work and my humanitarian heart kept us in a perpetual state of ever-increasing restlessness at our own inability to help. We did our best to compartmentalize in order to enjoy our honeymoon in Morocco. However, each night we tuned back in. CNN International, Al Jazeera, and the BBC became the soundtrack in our hotel rooms.

And quietly each night I would cry just as I did on that night in Germany. For the pain of those unjustly persecuted, for the gluttony of my own privilege, and for the gratitude I owe to the universe for allowing me this moment. Triggered by the heroes in Ukraine but unleashing pent up pain I felt for so many others.

Back on the trek, the sun rose the next day, and we left Pheriche through a wide valley. Unlike other parts of the trail, this section felt vast and endless. This stretch of trek was perhaps the loneliest of the trip. The wind was fierce, making the trek a slow trudge. I could feel my skin begin to chap from sun and wind. The wind's howl the only sound as the hours passed like molasses.

There is a saying in customer service training that you might be experiencing someone for the first time on the worst day of their lives. It is simply the idea that we do not know what we do not know. What would life be like if we could read people's souls so authentically. Would we offer others more grace, more empathy? Can we offer the same to ourselves?

This journey, literal and metaphorical, forced me to grow a deeper sense of self-empathy than I have ever known. As I took slow steps across the barren landscape, I let the tears flow without attempting to hide them or assign meaning. I just let them be.

We spend so much of our lives hiding our emotions, forcing ourselves to have only the emotional response appropriate for other's tolerance. While I believe emotional intelligence is critical for success, self-regulation is not the same as emotional repression. Real emotional intelligence is self-awareness and a deep understanding of our triggers. It's interacting with others from a place of calm truthfulness and genuine kindness. We may not always get it right. I certainly don't. But when you build upon a foundation of authenticity and look through a lens of empathy, we can build trust, foster communities, and raise up others. And that community will show up when we feel broken.

Chapter 12:
Khumjung

Altitude: 3,780m/12,402ft
Travel Time: Five to six hours walk
Soundtrack: I AM WOMAN, Emmy Meli

As the trail descends, the travel is easier and faster in pace. We arrive at Phunke Tenga after following the same trail back, passing by places like Pangboche, Deboche, and Tengboche.

Heading downwards and crossing a suspension bridge over the Dudh Koshi River, this trek onwards to the Khyangjuma is well-known as the trinity of ways to Gokyo Valley, Khumjung village, and Namche Bazaar. Views of peaks like Ama Dablam, Thamserku, Tawache, and Lhotse are stunning from here. Animal species common in the rhododendron forest are Pheasants, Himalayan Griffons, Musk deer, and wild goats and we search for sightings of all these creatures before reaching Khumjung for an overnight stay.

We are back under the tree line and the path is winding and serene, yet steep. A small misstep and I go careening down a slick portion, getting both bloody and dirt stained. A rush of hot tears fills my eyes, quickly overtaken by a fit of giggles. I brush myself off, reveling in the authenticity of getting dirty. Its day nine without a shower and somehow the uncomfortable has become comfortable. If you would have asked my childhood self if I was the kind of girl that could revel in the grittiness that is earned dirtiness, I would have scoffed. How far my life has come from that precocious little girl in a big white bow.

Getting Dirty

As a child, I had an aversion to being uncomfortable. Preferring the cool air-conditioned living room with dolls or books to the hot, muggy, backyard or playhouse. Preferring the college library to the intramural field and the corporate office to the field work. And then one day, it all changed. It started with a run and then another and another. As the miles passed, the sweat glistened. Then a visit to a flea market brought me to a piece of furniture my heart felt needed saving. Endless days were spent in my garage with a sander or a paint brush in hand, my face covered in dust and the occasional varnish stripe. There were weekends spent biking along Bayshore or doing yoga in the park. The sun's heat combined by the heavy blanket of Florida humidity in the air. Eventually, the Inca trail and this trek to Everest Base camp. Ever so slowly, the very thing I recoiled from, the gritty discomfort of dirtiness, became not simply a thing I endured but an addiction to replace all others.

They say you cannot grow until you face the uncomfortable. One yoga guru gave it a human-like character, saying you must sit in a room playing a child's staring game until it looks away first. Yet society teaches us to steer clear of the uncomfortable. To avoid situations that

186

could be unsafe. To shrink away from uncertainty. To sidestep topics that make others uncomfortable. To avoid saying any words we must muster the courage to say. And topping the list of forbidden topics: money, religion, death, and of course, sex.

Sex is everything and nothing all at once. It is the basic proliferation of humanity. It is an act of intimacy for a lifetime or a micro act of pleasure, easily forgotten. It is a tool to bring people closer or a weapon to tear people apart. It is an act of love or an act of hate. It can be beautiful or devastatingly ugly. It can be sensual and natural or frenetic and awkward. It opens treasure chests of pleasure or closes doors forever. If you have lived long enough or free enough, you might have experienced it all.

Growing up in a don't-ask-don't-tell family, no one gave me the sex talk. In fact, no one spoke of sex at all. Anything I knew about sex came from friends, Hollywood, or the even more confusing religious doctrines like saving yourself for marriage with a wink acknowledging no one really did.

I was a teen in the late '90s where condoms were prevalent, and the AIDS epidemic was still front and center. But freedom of sexuality was never discussed. So, I began early to associate sex, even the thought or curiosity of it, as shameful.

> *American culture is obsessed with purity. Purity obsession is directly correlated to sexual shame, and part of that obsession is how many sex partners you've had, aka your "number."*
>
> *We can be shamed for having "too much" sex or "too little" sex. Rarely does the shaming correlate with our actual sexual habits, but rather the assumptions people make about our sex lives and integrity, or the expectations we place on ourselves.*

Allison Moon, Getting It: A Guide to Hot,
Healthy Hookups and Shame-Free Sex, pg. 25-26

Couple this shame with a childhood need to be "seen" by men and the social lubricant of alcohol and my contaminated relationship with sex was perhaps the heaviest box to unpack.

In college, I alternated between empowerment and shame. I loved nearly everything about my college experience. From the sorority girls who became my second family to my job as a Disney character to my chosen major of organizational communications and rhetoric. It was the place I found my voice, in both writing and speaking. It was place I grew from a child from a small town to a young woman with individual values and passions. The only dark spot revolved around sex.

> *We don't shame people for visiting too many countries, for seeing too many movies, or having to many friends. Why is it a problem to have a large number of sex partners? Having a large sexual history means you have a wealth of knowledge about other people's bodies and desires. Experience is a virtue.*

Allison Moon, *Getting It: A Guide to Hot,
Healthy Hookups and Shame-Free Sex*, pg. 28

This is how I should feel about my early sex life. Like every other aspect of that chapter in life, I should embrace it as a time of growth and healthy experimentation. After all, I worked two jobs, held leadership roles in multiple organizations on campus, did philanthropy work, and maintained a *mostly* A GPA. I barely had time for sex, much less relationships where the idea of sex would somehow be socially accepted. But I was young and human. So, sex happened. Good sex, bad sex, drunk sex, pity sex. The joy of it all clouded by the farcical hypocrisy of traditional Christian values. The idea that sex has to be tied to marriage or at least love. The idea that practice makes perfect in every place except the bedroom. I was, and in some ways will always be, programmed to believe that sexual freedom is something to feel shame around.

The worst part of this particular shame is how much energy it wasted. If only I would have known that a decade later I could have better used that foundation of sexual empowerment to overcome a real sexual trauma.

Intuition Earmuffs

It was supposed to be a quick stop to enjoy the afternoon sun with a drink and my journal after lunch at the Grille with an old friend. I was seated at the rail overlooking the US Treasury building in the rooftop bar of a hotel just up the block from the restaurant. The weather was warmer than predicted, and just a few pages in, I found myself shifting uncomfortably trying to maintain a shady spot. Giving up, I turned to look for a table away from the ledge and in that moment locked eyes with two men.

They were well-dressed, one in a tan suit and collared shirt with one too many buttons undone. The other in dark jeans and a navy blazer with leather elbow patches. Both in shoes with a recognizable European flair. Packing up my things, I moved toward a shady table just on the other side of them. As I passed, Patches grabbed my arm.

"You are welcome to join us if you wish." His voice was deep with a thick English accent. I smiled shyly and declined.

With headphones blaring, I resumed writing. A few minutes later, I saw the waitress bring over a bottle of Veuve Clicquot accompanied by three glasses. I wondered if the third was for me but then laughed at my own presumption. However, no sooner had the thought crossed my mind, the waitress brought over a full glass. I looked up to see them raising theirs to me.

My sense of reciprocity obligation mixed with the treat of my absolute favorite champagne eventually overtook the judgmental finger wagging of my gut instinct, and I made my way to their table. They were in town for some apparent diplomatic purpose. Or so they said. DC is a town equally full of fake pretention as authentic importance. To me it made no difference as I have long stopped being impressed by accolades and credentials. Besides, I was in a headspace only half present in the conversation, the rest swimming in past emotions.

When my glass was empty, I made a feeble attempt to leave, to return to my "work," as I told them. But the refills were abundant, and I began to delight in the banter and laughter. Two hours and three bottles later both my head and my gut were screaming at me to get out of there. The tone of the conversation had become overtly sexual mixed with subtle forcefulness making my genuine laughter turn to uncomfortable, awkward smiles.

At last, I found my own firm voice, thanked them graciously, and stood to get a cab back to my conference hotel. Upon standing, however, my own weakness was exposed. I was baby deer stumbly, and my head ached with such ferocity that I had to squint my eyes from the light. Despite my protests, they insisted on accompanying me down to the lobby. I glanced nervously at the waitress who appeared to read my displeasure but decided against making a scene.

Just get downstairs, into a Lyft, and back to my own hotel for a nap, I told myself.

As we stood awaiting the elevator, I unconsciously began rubbing my temples. Noticing, Patches inquired and I mentioned the headache, just as the elevator arrived. As we stepped in, I saw he hit a floor far above my intended destination of lobby.

Me: Can you hit L for me please?

Patches: We'll stop by our room and get you some Advil for the long ride.

Me: That's ok. I am fine.

Tan Suit: We insist.

In that moment, a feeling swept over me that I instantly recognized.

Stopped in my Tracks

I was fourteen years old and taking voice lessons from our church's choirmaster. Once a week, I would walk from school to his church office for my lesson before being picked up by my mom to head home for dinner. It is hard to fathom how a place of such seeming innocence can become so dark.

For weeks, when my lesson concluded, I overheard him tell my mom he would be happy to take me home in the future. After all, he reasoned, he lived in a neighborhood just moments from ours. Eventually, frazzled by chaffering me five nights a week between two dance studios, theatre rehearsal, choir practice, and voice lessons, she agreed.

Even at fourteen, I knew the energy of that day felt different. He seemed nervous, distracted. When he called an end to our lesson I glanced at the clock. *Seven minutes early*, I thought, *that is weird*. His tendency was always to keep me late.

Nevertheless, we packed up and headed to his car, a small convertible. My hair was blowing around wildly as we sped down the highway, and I silently cringed as he reached over to touch it. Something about his hand in my hair felt wrong.

As we approached the entrance to my neighborhood, I realized he was in the wrong lane to turn. Inquiring, he assured me he just needed to stop by his house quickly before he took me home. Instantly my gut went from yellow flags to red. Why would he need to go by his own house when he would likely be headed there right after dropping me off? I began to fidget in my seat with visions of jumping out the passenger door. All I could think about was Genny.

Genny May Krohn, two years my junior, was a tomboy towhead blonde that lived down the street. While not close friends, we were part of the neighborhood kid squad that rode bikes and killed time together when our parents insisted on outdoor play. Until the day Genny did not come home.

In what can only be described as every 1990s parent's greatest fear, Genny was abducted at gunpoint while riding her bike in our own neighborhood, just steps from my front door. For three days and nights, hundreds of local residents searched woods and plastered flyers hoping for her safe return. The local, and eventually national, news carried the story. And parents like mine held their kids a little tighter at night.

On the third day, a highly unlikely miracle happened. The abductor got nervous and simply let Genny go. She made her way to a convenience store and called home. It was an unexpected happy ending but one that would change the face of our small community for years to come.

Back in the car with my voice coach, I rationalized that Genny's abductor was a stranger. This wasn't gun point; it was just a ride, I reasoned, I am making more of this than I should.

As we pulled into his driveway I sat up and firmly stated I would wait for him in the car. He seemed annoyed by this and calmly said he simply couldn't let me be alone, not after the recent kidnapping in the area. I secretly gawked at his seeming ability to read my mind, childish to not realize it had dominated the news.

Every hair stood up on the back of my neck as I stepped out of my car and made my way to his front door. I stepped one foot through the threshold and something unknown stopped me in my tracks. He spent several minutes trying to coerce me to close the door and come inside. He offered invitations to tour the house, have a lemonade, sing at his grand piano—all of which I declined. Staying firmly planted in the open doorway, his exasperation grew. I just kept repeating, "no thank you. I'd just like to go home. No thank you, I'd just like to go home." After twenty agonizingly long minutes, he eventually complied with my request, speaking not a word the entirety of the ride.

In the months that followed, he found dozens of excuses to cancel our voice lessons and abruptly decided to assign the lead role in our upcoming theatre production to someone else. On our annual musical tour, he all but ignored me, choosing instead his next protégé to dote over. The retaliation was crystal clear, and yet I was far too young to understand it. I told no one, as I felt I had nothing to tell. I simply absorbed the incident. At times, I mentally beat myself up with guilt about being so resolute. Was this my fault? Had I been too rude? Hadn't he been my coach and advocate for years? Wasn't he a kind, married, church choirmaster?

A decade later, I am drinking beers in the Bahamas on Spring Break with my college crew when the phone rang. My mom seemed frantic. "You should sit down," she said. I walked to the nearest woven plastic pool chair and did just that.

"He has been arrested." She stammered in tears that resembled hysterics. My former voice coach, arrested for child sexual assault and pornography. I sat stunned. Then a sense of relief slowly crept through my soul. I knew it. I fucking knew it. Turns out, I was not that ungrateful, rude child I had believed myself to be for the last decade. In fact, I was a child of intuition who very likely saved herself from a sexual predator.

The Elevator

The elevator bell dinged loudly as the doors opened eleven stories above the hotel lobby. What happened next is a blur. My slight frame was no match for the two of them at any time, but particularly not as drunk as I was at that moment. The video of this incident would surely look like helpless flailing rather than fruitful fighting.

Memories of trauma often become a series of scene flashes that do not necessarily connect in a methodical way. But what you do remember, you never forget.

I remember my head smacking loudly against the wall of the elevator as I aggressively backed away from them. I remember their hands on me, pulling at my blouse, reaching under my skirt, groping me, while I swatted uselessly and cursed at them.

"Get the fuck off me!"

I remember one pulling my hair in an attempt force me out of the elevator. Holding a self-taught degree in domestic violence, I knew enough about hotel attacks to know high-end hotels always turn the other cheek to loud screams or any "unsuitable chaos."

I don't remember how far their room was from the elevator but seemingly in an instant we were at the room door. Patches had a hold of my flailing arms as they pushed me through the threshold and onto the foyer floor. While I had known from the start that I was in danger, the sight of Tan Suit standing over me and Patches putting his hand over my mouth was the adrenaline rush I needed. I bit down hard on his hand, sending him recoiling for just the split second I needed to break free and run back for the door and down the hall.

"Dumb bitch," he scowled.

I looked around for the stairs but quickly realized I had run the wrong way. I took my chances hitting the elevator button instead and held my breath for their approach. To my surprise the elevator was still there and it appeared they hadn't followed me. I walked in and frantically began hitting buttons, any buttons to get the doors to close.

When the doors reopened to the lobby, I couldn't bring myself to say a word to anyone. I never stopped to talk to hotel security. I was vaguely aware of people staring at my tattered clothing and flushed face but stared blankly forward and walked directly out the doors of the hotel and into the street without looking back.

A car horn brought me back to reality as I nearly stepped into traffic. I turned on the sidewalk and nearly ran four or five blocks before leaning up against a building to catch my breath. Digging in my purse, I pulled out my phone to order a Lyft back to my hotel and caught a glimpse of my reflection. Smoothing down my tussled hair, I stared at the smeared makeup, bloody nose, and red mark across my cheek. Looking down, I caught sight of the scratches on my arms and red marks that would eventually turn purple. Suddenly the gravity of it all hit me like a ton of bricks.

The Lyft ride back to the Wharf felt a million miles long. I was spiraling into shame. I should have known better. I should have followed my gut. Don't drink so much. Don't drink with strangers. My gut knew something was amiss. I could have made a million different decisions. I could have been more forceful to say no to the offer in the first place. I could have left earlier. I could have slipped out and pretended to go to the bathroom. I could have signaled to the waitress. What happened to that childhood intuition that saved me once before? Had I become too accustomed to pleasing people? Was I so worried about being perceived as rude, that I could not stand my ground as I had as a child? Did I need attention so much I was willing to ignore my gut knowing I was in danger?

Claiming Sexuality

That afternoon changed my relationship with men for a very long time. Before that, I had certainly had sex I wouldn't repeat. People I wasn't really attracted to. People who weren't good humans. Nights I drank too much and going home with the person paying me attention seemed better than going home alone. But I made those decisions willingly, and I owned whatever consequences or emotions they evoked afterward.

This was different. No matter how much blame I wanted to place on myself, no matter how long I wanted to wallow in the shame of my own decisions, this was assault and not my fault. It took me years to say that sentence. In fact, it took me six years to ever mention this incident to anyone.

Whether sex happens during intentional acts of choice or unwanted traumas, our culture teaches us to hide it. To blame victims, gaslight accusers, repress memories, shame fantasies, and persecute anything that deviates from the pure, non-sin Christian version.

> *Sexual shame is a cycle beginning with a dominant cultural message that's internalized by the people of the culture and used to police their peers. At its most effective, sexual shame only needs an occasional nudge by those in power to keep it circulating through a community.*

> *At its most extreme, sexual shame encourages people to join hate groups, enact freedom restricting legislation, and commit violence against those who stimulate their feelings of self-loathing. Sexual shame prevents victims from reporting sexual crimes, talking frankly with friends and lovers about their desires and acknowledging and healing their trauma. It is, to be perfectly frank, what keeps us from being fully self-actualized humans.*

Allison Moon, Getting It: A Guide to Hot, Healthy Hookups and Shame-Free Sex, pg. 25

Sex is nothing if not a complicated dance between our physical, emotional, and psychological needs, all overlaid with ingrained societal norms of love and monogamy. All too often, this intertangled web leads to unrealistic relationship expectations of "having it all" or feeling that something is missing.

In, by far, my favorite Netflix series of all-time, *Sex/Life*, the main character, Billie, goes to see her former Columbia psychology professor to discuss her struggle with the 85/15. She has an enviable life with a loving husband, financial stability, and two healthy children—the 85%. And yet, she still feels a deep sense of lack. Of being invisible, undesired, trapped, and unable to fully express herself and her own sexual identity. She begins to fantasize about a long-lost love that held all the sexual excitement and danger but was volatile and unhealthy as a relationship—the 15%. Her advisor then states a truth that stopped me in my tracks.

> *"The person who gives you all that security can't also be the same person that gives you the thrill, the risk, the excitement, the lust—it doesn't work that way."*

Society would have us believe sexual enjoyment is only for the young or the reckless. That we are supposed to close that chapter when we grow up. That to be an adult means to give up part of ourselves. But this simply cannot be the truth. We should always want it all. We should always want to feel desired and adventurous. Perhaps being an adult simply means we have to work harder to get there.

The demons from my younger years have blessed me with a resolve to create an intentional healthy sex mindset. Regardless of the societal shame that surrounds it, I know if I can break the cycle, and embrace my own sexuality, I can transform my life.

Real sex, good sex, is a fully immersive experience. It's physical attraction, sure. But it's more than that. It's intellectual and spiritual as well. It's a dance of connective energy intertwined just right in that moment. And if you are lucky, that energy circulates between two people often enough or powerfully enough to be fully comfortable and open. Then it's not just sex—it's shame free, undeniable magic.

I believe we owe it to ourselves to become sexually free. Whatever that means for us individually. We can stay celibate for life or sleep with everyone we find interesting. We can follow the teachings of our chosen religion or follow our own sensuality. We can find the one and settle down or stay forever wild and free. We can have sex with men or women or both at the same time. We can get loud or stay demure. We can have all of this and a million other versions of a sex life completely shame free. The only thing that matters is our own self-awareness and self-love.

If we use sex to distract from other areas lacking in our life or our psyche, then it's time to stop and focus on those instead. If we use it as a crutch to make up for inadequacies in our self-esteem, then we must reinforce our own confidence first. If we drag into the bedroom sexual trauma from our past, it's time to lay that down outside the door. To be truly sexually free, we have to use sex for all its beauty and none of its pain. We must come to see it as a private reflection of exactly who we want to be, even if just in that moment.

There is so much work to be done in our society to normalize these ideas about sex. And it isn't likely in my lifetime. But if we get comfortable enough in our own bodies and minds, we can shift the experience of sex from forbidden and shameful to joy and ecstasy.

These days, when I am in DC, I walk past that hotel and gauge how much emotion it evokes. For years, I would instantly begin to feel nauseous. However, as the years have passed and I have finally started talking about it, the demons seem to be fleeting. My unconscious fear of being alone with men in elevators has subsided. The idea of being pushed up against a wall out of passion has stopped being a taboo experience. I've stopped letting tan suit and leather elbow patches ruin the beauty of my own sexuality.

Back on the trail, I brush off the dirt from my legs and begin again down the steep switchbacks. As devastating as my own experience was, I am well aware of how lucky I was to escape true harm a second time in life. I look down at my hands, with dirt under my nails and smudges on the palms, my knees scraped and bloody, and I simply say thank you for all of it. These hands, these legs, this body with all its imperfections remains strong and beautiful. But even more beautiful is my own intuition. It has never failed me; only I have failed it.

Chapter 13:
Return to Namche

Altitude: 3,440m/11,286 ft.
Travel Time: Five to six hours walk
Soundtrack: Lose Yourself, Eminem

Descending from Khumjung, we visit Khumjung Gompa, Khunde Hillary Hospital, and Government Yak Farm in the Khumjung valley. Crossing near Syangboche airstrip, the world's highest air strip, we walk towards Namche, reunite with the full group, and begin the celebration. We have done it.

It's hard to imagine missing out on this opportunity because of fear. Sure, I have plenty of fears—about failure, about losing loved ones, about being enough. But I no longer am afraid of trying new things, exploring new places, or doing just about anything that is tempting enough to turn my head.

Collection of Cages

"We hold the keys to the cages we build around ourselves."

This phrase was uttered casually, without contemplation, when I was put on the spot for a signature piece of advice. It was a chilly hotel ballroom at a speakers' conference in Sioux Falls, South Dakota.

Over time, I began to unpack the box of relevance to this statement. I saw examples everywhere I turned. With each piece of mounting evidence, I found validation. My resolve grew fierce to uncover it, to speak about it, to help others see and overcome it.

There is my childhood best friend. One of the most talented actresses I have ever known. Her talent trumped only by her character and grit. As children, we dreamed about life on a stage or, for me, in the writing room. And yet, neither of us followed that path. And both still itch for the chance. Many times, over the years we have reminisced about the "what if" and "if only." When we allow ourselves to look at the rearview mirror, we realize all the foundational blessings we both had which others did not. However, for both of us, we allowed parental expectations of what was a respectable career and a solid paycheck to outweigh our true talents and purpose. We both know deep down, however, the blame truly falls inward. We allowed upbringing to be an excuse to live in our fear. We quieted the voice in our heart and knot in our stomach with practicalities from our head. Maybe we would have failed but would the experience be any more painful than not trying? How much of the twenty-five years since we made that safe choice have we spent looking wistfully through the rearview instead of excitedly through the windshield?

There was a former co-worker, a brilliantly smart man with a loving wife, beautiful children, and a deep connection to his spiritual beliefs. A shining star with a young family and big aspirations. A jovial doer with solid values and pragmatic sensibility. He remained trapped in professional toxicity—all by choice. I watched as he squandered years of life under constant stress and anxiety, losing endless hours of laughter and joy with family, having vacations ruined by last minute demands on his time. As we drove over bridges in Portland on a work trip, I inquired about his professional journey. His response struck pings of sadness that reverberated with me for years to come. Although not his direct words, his sentiments reflected a sense of unworthiness, of insecurity, of being trapped by the financial incentives of his current position to such a degree he felt like he had no other option in life.

Another former co-worker admitted to the fullness of the misery yet lamented that it was "not as bad as the last place." How could a person of talent come to believe they are not worth more? How do we come to believe this was the best that life has to offer? What happens to make us believe a paycheck is more important than precious time with loved ones or even alone in life's glories? What allows us to believe manipulation and abuse is acceptable because it is attached to a career? Would we feel the same if we watched it happen to our spouse, child, or friend?

There were women in my professional circles who lived in perpetual waiting rooms. Their marriage unfulfilling but maintaining, their career unfulfilling but stable, their children well but detached. When the third glass of wine unlocks the trunk of melancholy, they admit to not living but simply existing. One thinks about divorce but stays only for her children. One would love to change careers but worries of the shock waves on her marriage. One longs to reinvent her relationship with her children but cannot break the obsessive devotion to her work. Each spends her days waiting for the next small joy to break up the weeks of monotony. How did this become their lives? When did obligation take the place of joy? What was once envisioned as life? Why had they allowed it to slip away like sand through fingers?

Perfectly articulated in her book *Called Out: Why I Traded Two Dream Jobs for a Life of True Calling*, Paula Faris discusses the idea of achievement addition. The idea that for some of us, from a very young age, achievement becomes our drug of choice. It seems like a positive trait for smart, ambitious kids. However, the ramifications of this behavior later in life often means we self-limit what we choose to do to only things we can excel at. For me, this need to be fail-proof sent me down a safe path has done more harm than good.

Each of these stories, and thousands more, illustrate cages we build around ourselves. For the years I wasted. For these souls and so many more. For those who have yet to complete construction on their cage. I stand at life's window screaming fiercely, *Look down, damn it. Look in your own hands and see the keys to freedom there.*

I came to this point myself, and I was faced with a choice. The career status I had strived so hard to obtain had become my own personal hell. Despite holding the power, I stood paralyzed wondering if life outside would really be better than the comfort of discomfort I was accustomed to.

I lamented these feelings to a close mentor who in an instant, changed everything for me.

"Can you do something that allows you to feed yourself? Do you have a roof over your head?"

"Yes," I replied.

"Then get out," he said. "Nothing else matters."

I was floored. This is a man who rose to the top of his $2.2 trillion company. And yet I recalled the time years earlier where he shared with me the story of his wealth gain, then loss, then gain again. It was a reminder that financial wealth is always at risk of failure. But the quality of our lives is within our control.

It was at that moment that I vowed not to remain locked inside cages of money, insecurity, fear, or simply melancholy habits.

In a sentiment articulated by author and facilitator Jen Pastiloff, when I get to the end of my life, I don't want my obituary to read "she worked really hard for a good salary" or "she toughed it out to fulfill financial goals" or "she settled for her mediocre job because it wasn't that bad."

No, I want it to say, "she was fearless in her pursuit to follow her dreams" and "she enriched the lives of others." I want to be remembered for the dirty hands and scrapped knees of being in the trenches serving the greater good. I want to be known as a woman who forged her own path and owned her own destiny.

But how do I ensure I am brave enough?

There is a lingering myth about elephants and thin rope. It is said that baby elephants were traditionally trained by tying a front leg to a stake in the ground. Because the elephants are small, only a thin rope is required. They'll struggle and pull at first, but eventually they realize that they can't break the rope and they'll give up. Over time, baby elephants become gentle giants however their memory and conditioning keep them from attempting to pull the rope, they never break free.

As a lover of (borderline obsessed with) elephants, I am not certain of the accuracy of this particular myth, but the meaning is nevertheless valid. Whether our cages are constructed from steel, gold, or string, we are likely to continue to reside in them without resistance until someone convinces us we are strong enough to break free. And most times, that person must be you.

It's 11:30 p.m.

The air was chilly as we sat in a rooftop bar in Albuquerque sharing whiskey cocktails and life stories. Taking turns, we swapped stories of marital struggles and advice on overcoming them. We lament the give and take that is inevitable, as no two people are so perfectly welded, they have no gaps for conflict. As we debate the merits of marriage and sacrifice, she says, "look at your parents—fifty years of marriage is such an accomplishment," and my visceral reaction is to cringe. It instantly dawns on me that this illustrates our lens on life is completely different.

My reaction represents nothing about my love for my parents or even my gratitude for never having to deal with the heartache and complications of a parental divorce. Both of these are deeply and authentically true for me. On the contrary, my reaction is personal and all about my definition of a cage.

To me, relationships are not an accomplishment to be admired. They are simply an exchange we make with another person. Like all choices in life. We are asking someone else to enjoy half the fun parts and bear half of the mundane parts of our lives in exchange for mutual singular attention. It's a choice we make to exchange freedom for security. It's a choice we make to give up potential life experiences for familiarity and stability.

For so many, particularly women, the idea of being without a relationship means being half looking for another half. They sit inside the cage of fear of their making. They see solitude as ugly and shameful, rather than beautiful and empowering. I believe I am a whole person all the time. I am fully capable and happy alone. If and when another person joins me and it is right for both of us, like meeting Randy, then that is a bonus. But I am still a complete person without him.

Believing that we need others to complete our lives keeps us locked in a cage of obligation and expectations.

> *You are in prison. If you wish to get out of prison, the first thing you must do is realize that you are in prison. If you think you are free, you can't escape.*

George Ivanovich Gurdjieff

In *The Crossroads of Should and Must: Find and Follow Your Passion*, Elle Luna posits,

> *We unconsciously imprison ourselves to avoid our most primal fears. Our prison is constructed from a lifetime of should, the world of choices we've unwittingly agreed to, the walls that alienate us from our truest, most authentic selves.*

So how do we know the difference? How can we be assured we are making choices based in authenticity and not obligation? That is something only you can know. All I can share is how it happened for me.

I started small. I took small risks and assessed the emotional damage when they failed. I tried new things, even if I had no experience or even good reason to do them. I made lists of things that simply intrigued me and spent the time, money, and effort to explore them. I simply listened to my intuition and allowed it to drive decisions even if no one else understood. And I didn't wait. I didn't wait for the *perfect* time, the *right* financial situation, or the *appropriate* companion. I simply took action. In the words of Lorne Michael, "We don't go on because it is ready. We go on because it is 11:30 p.m." And in my life, it is now always 11:30 p.m.

That night in Namche, we clink beers at the Irish bar as loud 1990s music blares. I look around as the drinks flow and night blurs, tasting the crisp and slightly bitter alcohol on my lips. It feels different than in the States. It feels earned. It feels honest. There is pure elation in the air with no hint of shame or escapism. What a difference a year has made.

Life is a journey. You can be in the fast lane, zipping through at the speed set by the cars around you, confined by societal expectations of worth based on other people's fears and insecurities. For me, I took the exit, wound down the country road, enjoyed the scenery, stopped at the farmers market, even forged my own way down a dirt road. The highway will always be there. I can get back on at any time. But just maybe I will never want to. Just maybe, the life I am designing is the life I was always meant to have.

Chapter 14:

Return to Lukla & Kathmandu

Altitude: 1,300m/4,264ft
Travel Time: Four-hour tarmac delay, an endless helicopter flight.
Soundtrack: I Lived, One Republic

The flash of the lightning is so close to the helicopter we have to squint at its bright light. It's pouring down rain and the forty-minute ride is now already over an hour with no end in sight. I am not really prone to panic but there is a sense of heightened awareness of the danger we are in. Our previous night of rabble-rousing coupled with the impending storm on its way to the mountain gave way to a group decision to obtain a series of helicopters from Namche to Kathmandu and avoid the final two days of trekking. This is a decision we would not regret. After the first ride out of Namche and a multi-hour wait on the Lukla tarmac, we were able to catch the final two helicopters of the day and leave the mountain. Brief moments after we were in the air, everything on the mountain shut down awaiting the hurricane force winds of the storm.

Despite the turbulent ride, we arrive safely in Kathmandu before the worst of it hits. We ride away in vans; soaked, tired, bruised and yet euphoric. We had said yes. Yes to one of the most challenging treks on earth. Yes to fear, to sickness, to exhaustion. Yes to vulnerability, to teamwork, to perseverance. We had said yes to ourselves, and not a one of us will ever be the same.

The last days in Nepal were spent nursing Randy back to health and frolicking in the local culture. We ventured to experience some of the most sacred and visited sights in the city. We shopped the local markets and ate the local cuisine. And then we wrapped with a farewell dinner in a typical Nepalese restaurant with live music. As we made our way to the airport to return to the States, I contemplated my life's call to action.

Run Molly, Run

Everything around me was covered in a thin sheet of tan dust including my eyelashes, which were now damp from tears. She is thirteen months old, lanky yet regal, a perfect shade of golden. And she is running. She is running at full speed for the first time in her life.

This book had been a figment in my imagination for a decade and a pile of ill-conceived notes and bullet points for four additional years. Having tried and failed at meaningful workday writing in my home office, I had come to Taos. To begin, to dive in, to write—with the subconscious acknowledgement that it would require opening a vault filled with chaos and frivolity and pain. Inside an imperfectly renovated 1950s airstream named Rosie, I shifted through the rubble for the treasures of life lessons and long forgotten smiles.

At my side sat Molly, my fifty-five pound Golden Retriever and Eva my thirty pound white mini-golden doodle. Eva, named after Everest, is my first dog and my first joint commitment with Randy. On our trek down from Base Camp, we vowed to find a puppy and name them after our journey. Eva if a girl and if a boy, Khumbu, after the Khumbu Glacier Everest sits on. A few weeks after arriving in Colorado, I found her. At the home of a small-town breeder in southeast Colorado, she was one of two puppies remaining, and in a twist of fate, already named Eva.

We call Eva our chubby party girl. She loves to sleep late, recognizes the sound of the strawberry fig bar wrapper from across the house, and sometimes doesn't jump quite high enough to make it onto the couch, sending her bouncing backwards. She is also my shadow, never leaving my side. Room to room in our home or off leash on a trail, she is never more than a few feet from me.

A year or so after Eva joined our family, we adopted five-month-old Molly from the Golden Retriever Rescue of the Rockies. While as playful as any puppy, she was never the innately bubbly stereotype of a Golden. With an air of an old soul, she kept a fairly solemn face at all times. She is also independent, loves attention but only on her terms. Lovingly known as our personal terrorist, she ate her way through over half my books, most every throw pillow and blanket in the house, and more than one round of computer cords and remote controls. Yet her sweet face and long eyelashes made her seem demure and innocent despite her mischief.

They accompanied me to Taos for a myriad of reasons: to keep me company, to test my ability to handle them on road trips alone, to keep them out of day camp for the week while Randy was at work. Little did I know how their presence would change everything.

We quickly fell into a new but natural rhythm of writing, research, walking, yoga, and play. We watched sunrises and sunsets. I poured over journal entries and old saved text messages. I sat in deep thoughts and quiet tears. From anger to shame, from disappointment to elation, I allowed myself to feel everything that arose without judgment. To relive each scene but through the lens of a voyeur, a journalist. What did I learn? How did it change me? What doors were opened from this?

On the second afternoon, creativity having hit a wall, I decided to take the pups farther out. The open space outside Taos is a beautiful mix of endlessly flat desert speckled with cactus and tumble weeds with the mountains standing in the distance like a picture-perfect postcard.

Just outside the park's perimeter I released them from their leashes and encouraged them to run. As predicted, Eva ran just a few feet away and stopped to wait for me. Molly, however, gave me one look to be sure it was OK and took off. Running about thirty meters away, she turned and looked for my approval again. I nodded in confirmation. This cycle repeated itself for the few minutes, each time her expression a little less solemn, even a hint of a smile. And then it happened.

Molly took off running at full speed. Across the desert landscape, her long legs in a fully extended gallop. She circled the cactus and zig zagged through scrub brush. She ran straight out and back in close stirring the dust around my legs. Every so often she would stop and look back at me, with puffed out ears and a smile I had never seen previously. And then she would begin again.

We repeated this ritual every few hours for the rest of the trip. And on that last morning, just before departure, something clicked. This is the first time in her entire life she has been able to do what she is built to do. The first time she has had the space and freedom to be the complete creature she is made to be. Born in a kennel, moved to the tiny apartment of her first owners, then landing with us where she has a backyard only big enough to make a few strides with those long legs before hitting a fence.

I stood frozen in awe—of her speed, her grace, and her sheer delight. It was a living metaphor for my own life. Of the daily fight to live the precise life I was meant to live, to be the person I am made to be.

The first time I formally put pen to paper for this work, I was sitting on my 28th floor balcony overlooking the Hillsborough River and the green grass of Curtis Hixon Park below. I had just completed Stephen Cope's *The Great Work of Your Life* for the third time. I closed it and sat in silence. Perhaps the third time will always be the charm for me as this read hit me completely different.

> *"What do you fear most in this life? What is your biggest fear? Right now. When I pose that question to myself, the answer is this: I'm afraid that I'll die without having fully lived."*

This opening line has never left my psyche. Living fully can mean a million different things unique to each one of us. In his work, Cope references it as dharma. Whether we call it dharma, God's calling, ikigai, raison d'etre or the like, nearly every culture and modern religion has a reference to a concept similar. Despite distinctive differences in detail, the overarching concept remains: being the human we are meant to be. Living a full life as our full selves.

Not dissimilar to a cheetah named Tabitha in Glennon Doyle's *Untamed*, in that desert valley I saw that illustration take on life. Deep, uninhibited joy seen through a dog simply living her dharma. One that feels like home even through the grittiness.

Molly ran hard. And then she was tired. She was thirsty. She was dirty. She needed rest. But then, she got up, shook off the dust and did it all over again. And the joy returned. Isn't that how we all want to live our lives?

The Ripples We Leave

As I sat day after day, week after week to write this work, I thought about the vast network of souls who have enriched this thing I call a life. Those I was brave enough to sit face-to-face and articulate what they meant to me and those who may never know. Those that earned ink here and those that are only in my heart.

> *Sometimes I am boggled by the gallery of souls I have known. By the lore. The wild history, unsung. People crowd in and talk to me in dreams. People who died or disappeared or whose connection to my own life makes no logical sense, but exists, as strong as ever, in a past that seeps and stains instead of fading. But sometimes the million stories I've got and the million people I've known pelt the roof of my internal world like a hailstorm.*

Rachel Kushner,
The Hard Crowd; coming of age on the streets of San Francisco.
The New Yorker January 2021

In his iconic Ted Talk, Dan Pollatta expounds an epic truth: "People are yearning to be asked to use the full measure of their potential for something they care about." We all want to run at full speed. What holds us back? More often than not, it is fear—of the unknown, the unfamiliar, the uncomfortable. Other times we simply do not know where we are supposed to be or how to get there.

In *The Top Five Regrets of the Dying*, Australian author Bronnie Ware writes the lessons she heard consistently from her time caring for people on their deathbed. Regrets of having conformed to the expectations of others therefore not being true to themselves. Regrets of prioritizing work over family. People who wished they spoken up more, said I love you more. Those that wished they had stayed in touch with old friends. And most of all, those that wished they had allowed themselves to be happier. They had been content, but ultimately they would have liked to have laughed more, to have been more lighthearted and let their hair down more authentically.

Only at the end of our lives do we realize that being happy is an actual choice. Perhaps if we spent more time with family and friends, told people we loved them even when it was scary, and stopped being hemmed in by social conventions and fear of change, we would, in fact, be happier. So perhaps that is where this starts—saying the words on the tip of our tongue that we have never been brave enough to utter. Making sure our time is prioritized in a way that reflects our individual values. Doing the things and surrounding ourselves with the people that bring us the greatest joy and nothing less.

There are moments in life where we are led, seemingly subconsciously, to say things, do things, or embark on adventures out of our comfort zone or character. Sometimes we go along willingly, and sometimes we resist and always regret it. A 3:00 a.m. purchase of bright red pointe shoes during the pandemic reignited a creative side that led to richer memories to write about. A spontaneous flight to DC for the 2017 Women's March with no planned place to sleep led to a fierce passion to protect the path for other women including the nieces that are my only legacy. Taking my chances as an entrepreneur led to the richest career experiences I could have ever known. Taking a sixteen-day trek to a famous glacier led to the bravery and vulnerability to share these stories.

> *The greatest legacy we leave is that of our presence, our authenticity, and the rippling effect we have had on the people we meet, the initiatives we were involved in and the work we did. If we have been able to be with people in their joys and their despair, if we have opened metaphorical doors for others in our personal life or our professional capacities, if we have been a mensch, as the Yiddish expression goes, this is our legacy.*

Lionel Shriver, "Be here Now means gone later,"
Selfish, Shallow, and Self-Absorbed;
Sixteen Writers on the Decision Not to Have Kids, pg. 194

I once thought the goal was to turn my incongruence, my dharma adjacent life, into something I called becoming congruent. What I discovered along the way is that I don't need to become anything. I just need to own my life for exactly what it is. Incongruent…with societal norms on religion and sex, with previous notions of who I would love, with white picket fence lifestyles, and with the parental path of others.

I have long believed that every human has a story worth telling. Our authentic life experience is a winding path that is both beautiful and unsightly but always unique. There will be some who can recognize this for themselves. But far fewer will find a way to share these scenes more broadly for all to see.

For me, I made the decision to share. To you, some of this might simply be words on a page, too unconnected to your reality to hold space in your psyche. However, my gut says some of this will hit home. Whether a story, an emotion, or an inspiration, in my gut I believe there are connection points that will serve as validation for your own experiences or legitimation of your own decisions. And my gut is never wrong.

And thus, I have made this collection of life stories part of my legacy. To tout the mantra of living life on your own terms and being brave enough to push into uncomfortable. Life is all about decisions, and those decisions individually and cumulatively create the life that we have. Some may hold more benefit and some, more sacrifice, but we should never underestimate all that will grow over time from each decision we make. Every choice is a tradeoff and the best we can hope for is to get it right as often as possible.

If I could leave one sentiment behind when I leave this earth it would be this: While we cannot always change our circumstances, we can always change our perspective. Nothing in life is permanent and nothing in life is truly under our control. So why not just be whoever we want to be. Its neither too late nor too early to live the life you dream of. It is neither too late nor too early to find the Molly of your own life. Start by simply saying yes. Say yes to the things that we fear. Say yes to the people we love. Say yes to what lights up our soul. Say yes. Every. Damn. Time.

Make your dream devour your life, so that life does not devour your dream.

Antoine de Saint-Exupery

217

Acknowledgments

They say it takes a village to raise a child. It also takes a village to raise a soul. The words in this book represent individual pieces of my heart that could never have seen the light of day without the support and encouragement of so many. Thank you...

To Randy: Thank you for steadfastly believing in me and this work. For giving me the space to be vulnerable about chapters of life that far predated our intertwining. And for eventually believing I was just tall enough.

To Mom and Dad: I am the luckiest child in the world to be born to two of you. Your love and endless support has made me the woman I am. May this work and my entire life be dedicated to making you proud.

To my brother, sister-in-law, cousins, nieces, and extended family: While I have managed to continue to be the independent soul that both scares and befuddles you, thank you for always providing the foundation of support I needed to know I am loved.

To Devin and Anthony (aka TnT): Thank you for being my ride-or-dies, my football buddies, my no-judgement-zone group text saviors, and my endless encouragers and cheerleaders. While neither of you may ever read this work, you have never let me give up on it. I know you always have my back.

To my Tampa besties Lana and Monica: I have been blessed to share miles of travel and years of life with each of you and I am truly a better person for it. I love you both forever.

To Jon: Six years ago, I was humbled to be your business mentor. Today I am humbled to be your mentee. Thank you for being an early reader. Thank you for pushing me to write the hard things. Thank you for helping me find ways to overcome the writer's block. Thank you for reminding me it is worth it.

To my Colorado "Fly Girls" Squad Nadine, Hayley, April: All three of you walked into my life as this work was being formed and your endless support for this and all life's chapters is priceless. Here's to more laughter, more wine, and more fly fishing.

To Sydney, Carrie, Erin: Each of you played such an important role in a particular chapter of my life. No words can fully express my gratitude for those years and for your enduring presence to this day.

To Roni, Liz, Jen, Jaime, Janice, Michelle, Megan, Bekah, Kaitlyn, Karinda, LPP, LTB013, Retreat Journey, Bella Prana, UT Lunch Bunch, and dozens of other friends who have loved and supported me over the years: I may not have ink to mention each of you here, but my heart is permanently imprinted with your love.

To the anonymous: For the nameless who earned ink in this work, you know who you are, and I thank you. Whether positive or challenging, your role in my life's story holds merit as part of the human experience.

To Jennifer Pastiloff: Your inspiration has been part of my soul since our first meeting. I am so blessed for your mentorship, your support and now your words attached to this work.

To the team that brought this work to life: Neon Pig Creative, Quail Run Editorial, Book Savvy PR, and Kayla O'Brien Media. You are a dream team to work with and I am so blessed you believed in this book.

To the places that stirred my soul to write, you will forever be a part of this journey.

Tattered Cover, Denver, CO

The Rosie, Taos, NM

The TJ Tower, Birmingham, AL

Serendipity Labs, Denver, CO

The Moxy, Austin, TX

Park Benches, New York City, NY

Lakeside Couches, Georgetown, GA

Morocco Tour Van, Winding streets throughout the country.

Airplane Seats, Thousands upon thousands of Miles through the Sky

About the Author

Melanie Sue Hicks is an adventure seeking, social impact advocate dedicated to helping others overcome fear and live their dharma. She has led or participated in service projects around the world and dedicates her life to creating impact on her own or amplifying the impact of others every single day.

As an empathy driven education, nonprofit and workplace expert, she has been interviewed and published in dozens of magazines and websites including Forbes.com, Marie Claire, Authority Magazine, See Beyond Magazine, Thrive Global, The District, and Doctor's Life Magazine. As an experienced motivational speaker and master facilitator she has used her custom 3E Method of Change© along with her unique style of group facilitation, to assist organizations navigate the future of education and work for increased retention, productivity, and revenue.

Made in the USA
Columbia, SC
20 March 2023

14026582R00130